HENRY DAVID THOREAU

A BIOGRAPHY

HENRY DAVID THOREAU

MILTON MELTZER

TFCB

Twenty-First Century Books
Minneapolis

Twenty-First Century Books
A division of Lerner Publishing Group
241 First Avenue North
Minneapolis, Minnesota 55401 U.S.A.

Website address: www.lernerbooks.com

Library of Congress Cataloging-in-Publication Data

Meltzer, Milton, 1915–
Henry David Thoreau : a biography / by Milton Meltzer.
    p.   cm.
Includes bibliographical references and index.
ISBN-13: 978-0-8225-5893-4 (lib. bdg. : alk. paper)
ISBN-10: 0-8225-5893-9 (lib. bdg. : alk. paper)
1. Thoreau, Henry David, 1817–1862—Juvenile literature. 2. Authors, American—19th
century—Biography—Juvenile literature. 3. Naturalists—United States—Biography—Juvenile
literature. 4. Intellectuals—United States—Biography—Juvenile literature. I. Title.
PS3053.M395 2007   818'.309—dc22 [B]   2006013747

Manufactured in the United States of America
1 2 3 4 5 6 – BP – 12 11 10 09 08 07

ALSO BY MILTON MELTZER

Contents

INTRODUCTION

In the days of Henry David Thoreau, few people beyond his hometown knew of his existence. He published only two books, and not many people read them. Yet now, nearly 150 years since his death, dozens of volumes quarried from his vast journal and his other writings have been published. His classic book, *Walden*, valued as one of the great works of American literature, has been translated into many languages. His essay "Civil Disobedience" has shaped the thought and actions of such leaders as Mohandas Gandhi and Martin Luther King Jr.

Yet in his own time and for quite a while afterward, people had the notion that Thoreau was just a layabout, spending his hours thinking "big" thoughts. A layabout? You'll see how hard he worked—as farmer, gardener, house painter, carpenter, mason, surveyor, pencil maker, day laborer, schoolmaster, lecturer, naturalist, and writer.

This book tells of his daily life, its ups and downs, what he wrote and why. And it tells of the way his creativity continues to influence and delight the world around us.

must have some complicated machinery or other, and hear its din, to
that idea of government which they have. Governments show thus bot
cessfully man...ance b...ten in...os... hemselves, for th

Chapter One

Every Bug, Bird, Berry, and Beast

HENRY DAVID THOREAU was born in a plain New England farmhouse on the outskirts of Concord, Massachusetts. The date was July 12, 1817, only some forty years after Thomas Jefferson wrote the Declaration of Independence. Concord, then a village of about two thousand people, is seventeen miles northwest of Boston—four hours by stagecoach then. With Lexington, it shares the honor of being the birthplace of the American Revolution.

In Thoreau's time, Concord was a trading center for farm and garden products. Here the famous Concord Coach, the stagecoach often seen in Western movies, was manufactured. The town would gain its most lasting fame, however, as the home of several of America's most distinguished writers.

Henry's father, John Thoreau, of French Protestant origin, was a storekeeper for many years. Later he took up manufacturing pencils, a business in which Henry would join him. Henry's mother, of Scottish heritage, was the former Cynthia Dunbar. The

When Henry was about a year old, the Thoreaus left the farm where he had been born. After many owners, the farm was eventually scheduled for demolition and development. In 1992 a group of Concord citizens known as the Thoreau Farm Trust purchased the property, which has been restored as an education center.

couple had three children besides Henry: Helen first, then John Jr., Henry (born David Henry, but later changed to Henry David) next, and finally, Sophia.

The first Thoreaus to come to America arrived in Boston in 1773. (The name is pronounced with the accent on the first syllable, as in "furrow.")

Henry's family knew hard times early on as his father struggled to make a living. But despite years of poverty, Mrs. Thoreau's skills as housekeeper and cook and her generous heart and keen mind made for a happy family life. She would always find a way to help those poorer than herself. Everyone was welcome in her home. She was known to be a great talker, never afraid to speak her mind on the social and political issues the nation confronted.

Henry's father, John Thoreau (left), *storekeeper and pencil maker, was of French Protestant descent. The only existing likeness of Henry's mother, Cynthia Dunbar Thoreau, is this cut-paper silhouette. Cynthia was the daughter of a New England clergyman.*

Her support of the antislavery cause led the family to give shelter to fugitive slaves bound for Canada and freedom.

Whenever they could spare the time, Henry's parents took long walks together in the fields and woods. Henry's friend Horace Hosmer believed that Henry's love of nature was transmitted from his parents.

Henry's older sister, Helen, was a quiet, retiring schoolteacher during her brief adult life. She died young of tuberculosis, the contagious lung disease that killed so many. John Jr. was a lively, outgoing youngster and the idol of his kid brother. Sophia, two years younger than Henry, worshipped Henry, sharing his interest in nature. She would often go along with him on his hikes and boat rides.

The Thoreau household was frequently filled to overflowing with relatives and friends. Later, to help make ends meet, the family took in boarders. Mrs. Thoreau was said to set the best table in Concord. Among the boarders were aunts as well as a bachelor uncle, Charlie Dunbar. He amused the family with all sorts of card tricks, though he didn't gamble. Dunbar often delighted his young nephew by tossing his hat into the air, turning it over and over, and then catching it on his head.

It was the same Uncle Charlie who led Henry's father into pencil manufacturing. While wandering around New Hampshire in 1821, he had found a graphite mine. He knew graphite was used to make pencils and established a claim to the deposit. Soon

John Thoreau's pencil company provided a good living for the family by producing an excellent product. The Thoreau name is prominent in the history of pencil making.

he and Henry's father set up shop in Concord to turn out pencils. When Uncle Charlie lost interest and dropped out, the business became know as John Thoreau & Co. When his pencils earned an award for their high quality, Henry's family no longer teetered on the edge of bankruptcy.

In Henry's early years, the family rarely stayed put in any one house. Sometimes it was only a matter of months before they had to shift to another. But no matter where he lived, to Henry, Concord was the center of the universe. "I have never got over my surprise that I should have been born into the most estimable place in all the world, and in the very nick of time, too," he wrote in 1856.

Henry attended a public grammar school at first. There was a two- or three-month winter session, with the teacher usually an undergraduate released from college to earn money for tuition. The tougher farmboys often fought, making discipline a serious problem. A woman teacher took over in the ten-week summer session, and mostly girls attended, for the boys were busy on the farm.

The school was overcrowded, so much so that girls were allowed in only for the elementary grades, to leave room for the boys. All grades were packed onto benches rising on tiers. The teacher sat at a raised desk down below. Only a few courses were offered. Reading and writing, a dip into some American history, arithmetic, and perhaps a bit of algebra. For the public speaking lessons, the reciting of poems and perhaps a comic piece would do.

In 1828, when Henry was eleven, he and brother John entered the Concord Academy. The tuition fee for this private school was five dollars a quarter per pupil, and with both boys going, it was a substantial sum out of the family budget. No matter: Mrs. Thoreau had a powerful desire to see her sons get the best education.

Henry was a good student, but not a mixer. He stood aside and watched when the others played games. Even when the townsfolk turned out for street parades and the rollicking music of bands, he would stay home. He liked to watch the canal barges move along the Concord River, loaded with bricks or iron ore, and was thrilled when the boatmen let him leap aboard for a short passage. A special treat came when his mother asked him to stay home from school to pick the huckle-berries she needed for a pudding. With her love of nature, she tried to open her children to its delights. Growing up in the countryside, Henry would come to know every bug, bird, berry, and beast, every fruit and every flower.

The classics were the heart of the curriculum at the Concord Academy. The boys studied poetry, drama, and prose in the orig-inal languages—Greek, Latin, and French. Other courses included grammar, spelling, history, geography, algebra, geom-etry, trigonometry, astronomy, botany, and natural history. Phineas Allen, the headmaster (who boarded at the Thoreaus'), required frequent writing on various themes. One of Henry's pieces, written around age eleven, survives:

The Seasons
Why do the seasons change? And why
Does Winter's stormy brow appear?
Is it the word of him on high,
Who rules the changing varied year?

Henry then goes on to describe in lyrical writing what he sees in the four seasons as they change. He was opening a path he would follow the rest of his life.

The headmaster launched a Concord Debating Society for his students as an extracurricular activity. Henry debated quite often but wasn't rated highly. Before the year was up, the Concord

Lyceum, a community education center featuring lectures on literary, historical, scientific, and moral themes, was founded. It was open to everyone. At first the lectures were given by local people, but soon speakers were exchanged with the many other lyceums springing up throughout the nation. Later on Thoreau would make lyceum talks a source of income and use them to spread his views.

Chapter Two

COLLEGE YEARS

IN THE SUMMER of 1833, after his final session at Concord Academy, Thoreau built his first boat, calling it *The Rover*. In it he rowed along Concord's rivers and floated dreamingly on Walden Pond. Such lazy days, he thought, made "idleness the most attractive and productive industry."1

He couldn't be lazy or idle for long. Four years at Harvard College lay ahead.

Thoreau wasn't eager to go. His father thought maybe it would be best to apprentice Henry to a carpenter. But no, said his mother. She wanted one of her boys to study at Harvard. Her own father did. Why not Henry? To meet the cost, everyone pitched in. The pencil business was off to a good start. Helen and John were teaching school and could offer help. The aunts boarding with them insisted on helping too.

How much was needed? Tuition was $55 a year, and adding textbooks and room and board, total expenses came to $179 a year. That sounds ridiculously inexpensive now. But think of average earnings for that time: a village school teacher earned $100 a year; a laborer on the Erie Canal, 88¢ a day; a carpenter, $1.25 a day. Back then it required all that the Thoreaus could scrape together to meet Henry's needs.

That summer Thoreau took the entrance exams and barely made it. As September 1833 began, he traveled the fifteen miles to Cambridge and settled into his room at Hollis Hall. The college at that time was just a small cluster of old brick buildings. There was University Hall for classrooms, the library, the chapel, and three dormitories. Cambridge itself was a small town, with unpaved but tree-lined streets and open fields and woods just beyond.

The oldest American college, Harvard was founded in 1636. It was still a small college, with most of the students drawn from

In addition to Thoreau, a number of other American literary greats were educated at Harvard (above), *among them Ralph Waldo Emerson and poets Wallace Stevens, e. e. cummings, and T. S. Eliot.*

nearby. Many freshmen were only fifteen, or even younger. Thoreau had just turned sixteen. When Thoreau entered, he took courses that had changed little since pre-Revolutionary War days. The classics were the heart of the curriculum, and the training was directed more toward preparing students for the ministry than for any other profession.

There were 432 students and twenty-five faculty members—a few of them with high reputations in their field. Thoreau's classes included English, Greek, Latin, mathematics, history, the sciences, philosophy, and theology.

Modern languages were optional. Although Thoreau did not have to take them, he was deeply interested in language and took several terms each in Italian, German, French, and Spanish. He learned to read them with ease, and it opened his mind to literature as a multicultural art.

In the spring of 1837, young Henry Wadsworth Longfellow, returning from two years of study in Europe, began to teach at Harvard. Thoreau sat in on Longfellow's lectures on language and literature. He found the professor's broad knowledge of poetry and the classics a stimulus to his own experiments in poetry and prose.

In his three years of English with Professor Edward T. Channing, Thoreau wrote many essays on assigned themes. The struggle to learn to express himself under Channing's tutelage proved helpful. His grades overall earned him an above-average ranking.

The goal of Harvard in Thoreau's time was not a liberal education but rather a "thorough drilling." A marking system that assigned points to every aspect of college life—including class recitation, themes, assignments, attendance at chapel, class or curfew violations, and any and all forms of misbehavior—was hated by the students. So much so that in the spring of 1834, toward the end of Thoreau's first year, a famous rebellion broke out. Thoreau did not take part in the rebellion, which began when a student said something insolent to a teacher and ended with rioting,

In the spring of Thoreau's senior year, he enrolled in a course in German literature, taught by Henry Wadsworth Longfellow. The young professor, not yet published, had recently returned from two years in Germany and Switzerland, where he had been studying languages and grieving over the death of his young wife.

costly damage to furniture, and smashed windows. Harvard president Josiah Quincy expelled the entire sophomore class.

Essays Thoreau wrote in his college years reveal his early belief in the individual's self-fulfillment. Society is only the means to that end, Thoreau felt, not the other way around. One theme he struck was, "We are apt to become what others think of us." Another of his concerns was, "The duties, inconvenience, and dangers of conformity." He believed, "The fear of displeasing the world ought not, in the least, to influence my actions." You must listen to your conscience, he insisted, or "the principal avenue to reform would be closed."

Harvard allowed students to drop out for a thirteen-week period of teaching in a secondary school. The aim was to earn money needed for tuition. From December 1835 into March

1836, Henry taught a class of seventy students at a school in Canton, Massachusetts. The best part of that job was the friendship he developed staying with Orestes A. Brownson (1803–1876), a young and fiery Unitarian minister who had children of his own in the school. Brownson was a keen thinker, and the two would sit up nights talking about the new reformist ideas circulating in New England.

That May, Thoreau began to feel so weak and exhausted that he was unable to resume his studies at Harvard. No diagnosis is on record, but it's likely this was the first time tuberculosis (called consumption then) attacked him. The medical records of Concord, and of Thoreau's own family, attribute more deaths to this plague than to any other cause. No one knew then the disease was contagious, and when the sick were not isolated, the disease would rage through the community. Physicians today believe Thoreau survived this attack and several more later because of his love of being outdoors every possible hour.

Some of the family thought that he ought to give up on Harvard, that his body couldn't stand the pressure. But he insisted he'd go back in the fall. During the summer, he built himself a new boat, "a kind of oblong bread-trough" with sails, as he called it. He named it *Red Jacket*.

With his father, he made a brief trip to New York to peddle their pencils in the stores. It would help pay the cost of his next term at Harvard. But back on campus in the fall of 1836, illness again set in, more than once. Luckily it was not so bad as to force him home again.

One of Henry's classmates, John Weiss, left us his impressions of Thoreau. He said his "prominent grey-blue eyes seemed to rove down the path, just in advance of his feet. His eyes were sometimes searching, as if he had dropped, or expected to find, something. It was the look of Nature's own child learning to detect her wayside secrets. . . . He saw more on the ground than anybody

*This drawing of Henry Thoreau was done by Samuel
Worcester Rowse (who would later become very well known)
during the summer of 1854 while Rowse was boarding with
the Thoreaus. Although Thoreau was thirty-seven at the
time, his youthful looks make this the only known portrait
that shows what he might have looked like as a young man.*

suspected to be there. His eyes slipped into every tuft of meadow
or beach grass, and went winding in and out of the thickest under-
growth, like some slim, silent, cunning animal. They were
amphibious besides, and slip under fishes' eggs and into their
nests at the pond's bottom, to rifle all their contents. . . ." He

added that Thoreau, with his prominent, curved nose, looked "very much like some Egyptian sculptures of faces, large-featured, but brooding, immobile, fixed in a mystic egotism."

Harvard's custom at that time was to schedule graduation in late August, preceded by a six-week summer vacation. Henry and his college roommate, Charles Stearns Wheeler, spent those weeks living in a shanty Wheeler had built at the edge of Flint's Pond in nearby Lincoln. They did nothing but read, loaf, and sleep. The rest might well have helped stave off another attack of tuberculosis for Thoreau.

Flint's Pond (also known as Sandy Pond) in Lincoln, Massachusetts, is located one mile (1.6 km) east of Walden Pond. Thoreau spent the summer here with Charles Stearns Wheeler. Thoreau later sought permission from farmer Flint to build his own cabin on Flint's Pond but was refused. So Thoreau built at Walden Pond instead.

Upon graduation on August 30, 1837, Thoreau received the degree of bachelor of arts. His rank in his class earned him a place on the commencement program. His speech was entitled "The Commercial Spirit of Modern Times, Considered in Its Influence on the Political, Moral, and Literary Character of a Nation." In it,

ORDER OF EXERCISES

FOR

COMMENCEMENT,

XXX AUGUST, MDCCCXXXVII.

Exercises of Candidates for the Degree of Bachelor of Arts.

[The performers will speak in the order of their names.]

1. A Salutatory Oration in Latin.
   CHARLES THEODORE RUSSELL, *Princeton.*

2. A Conference. "The Influence of Young's and Cowper's Poems."
   DANIEL WIGHT, *Natick.*
   WILLIAM PINKNEY WILLIAMS, *Baltimore, Md.*

3. An Essay. "The Effect upon Literature of a Belief in Immortality."
   JOHN FOSTER WILLIAMS LANE, *Boston.*

4. A Conference. "The Commercial Spirit of Modern Times, considered in its Influence on the Political, Moral, and Literary Character of a Nation."
   CHARLES WYATT RICE, *Brookfield.*
   DAVID HENRY THOREAU, *Concord.*
   HENRY VOSE, *Dorchester.*

5. A Literary Disquisition. "Modern Imitation of the Ancient Greek Tragedy."
   SAMUEL AUSTIN KENDALL, *Utica, N. Y.*

MUSIC.

6. A Dissertation. "Severity of Manners in a Republic."
   CLIFFORD BELCHER, *Farmington, Me.*

7. A Philosophical Disquisition. "The Real or Supposed Decline of Science at the Present Day."
   SAMUEL TREAT, *Portsmouth, N. H.*

Speaking assignments for the Harvard Class of 1937 were assigned on the basis of class standing. Mid-ranked seniors such as Thoreau, who was number nineteen in his class of forty-seven, shared orations. Thoreau was assigned the moral aspect of the three-part topic, "The Commercial Spirit of Modern Times, Considered in Its Influence on the Political, Moral, and Literary Character of a Nation."

he voiced a philosophy he would follow for the rest of his life:

> We are to look chiefly for the origin of the commercial spirit, and the power that still cherishes and sustains it, in a blind and unmanly love of wealth. Wherever this exists, it is too sure to become the ruling spirit; and, as a natural consequence, it infuses into all our thoughts and affections a degree of its own selfishness; we become selfish in our patriotism, selfish in our domestic relations, selfish in our religion. Let men, true to their natures, cultivate the moral affections, lead manly and independent lives; let them make riches the means and not the end of existence, and we shall hear no more of the commercial spirit. The sea will not stagnate, the earth will be as green as ever, and the air as pure. This curious world which we inhabit is more wonderful than convenient; more beautiful than it is useful; it is more to be admired and enjoyed than used. The order of things should be somewhat reversed; the seventh should be man's day of toil, wherein to earn his living by the sweat of his brow; and the other six his Sabbath of the affections and the soul,—in which to range this widespread garden, and drink in the soft influences and sublime revelations of nature.

The ceremony over, Thoreau headed back to Concord. What had he got out of college? Little, precious little, he would say in later years. But his studies there carried him beyond the narrow little world of Concord. He was exposed to new books and to fresh ideas. "And it honed his intellect to razor sharpness," said his biographer Walter Harding, one of the most eminent scholars of Thoreau.

Chapter Three

PENCILS AND PUPILS

THERE WERE FOUR PATHS to follow if you were a college graduate in that time: teacher, preacher, doctor, or lawyer. For Thoreau it was teacher. His father, grandfather, brother, sister, aunt—each had chosen to teach at one time or another. And no sooner had Thoreau taken his degree than Concord asked him to teach in the same public grammar school he had gone to ten years earlier. The salary would be one hundred dollars a year.

He was lucky to find work, unlike many of the men in his class. The first of many economic crises that would devastate America had begun. Many people had been gambling with investments, and business had grown increasingly shaky. Crop failures that spring hastened the economic collapse. Mechanics and laborers suffered badly. Prices for food and fuel shot up, and desperate people in the cities rioted in the streets. In New York, every third worker lost his job. Ten-year-old boys and girls labored in the mills of New England from dawn to dark at tasks often beyond their strength. They pocketed hardly more than a dollar a week. The effects of the economic depression would hang on for nearly seven years.

About fifty pupils ages seven to eighteen crowded the one-room schoolhouse each day. Restless horseplay and some fighting made discipline a problem at times. Two weeks into the term, one of the school committee members dropped by to see how Thoreau was doing. When he observed that some students were disrupting class and that Thoreau was not using corporal punishment to put a stop to it, he called him aside. You've got to punish those troublemakers, he said, or the school will fail.

As shocking as it seems in the light of today's laws regarding the treatment of students, in Thoreau's time, corporal punishment was considered a legitimate part of a teacher's educational arsenal.

That was not Thoreau's idea of good teaching. The cowhide may teach a truth in physics, he said, but never a truth in morals. To show how absurd the committee's rules were, Thoreau called out six of the pupils and hit each of them on the palm of a hand with a stick. The students were puzzled and angry. He had never done this before. He seemed the kindest of men.

That evening Thoreau quit his job. He had to teach in his own way or not at all.

That was the end of his teaching career in public schools. The Concord people couldn't understand anyone giving up a job, especially in these hard times. Hadn't children always been whipped for bad behavior? Why couldn't Thoreau do it? What was wrong with him?

Thoreau tried for many months but failed to find another teaching position. He got in touch with schools in New York, Virginia, Kentucky, and Maine. He would not sit around doing nothing, so he went to work in his father's pencil factory. Not a hard choice for it brought him closer to his father and at least now he was earning his own keep. American pencils were not much good: greasy, gritty, brittle. His mind always keen, Thoreau soon saw a way to improve the quality of their pencils. Researching at the Harvard library, he learned that the good German pencil makers mixed a certain Bavarian clay in with their graphite. He found that the clay was imported into America. He ordered a batch and worked out the mechanical means of integrating it into his father's production process. The result was the first American pencil as good as the best German product.

Thoreau also made a machine that drilled a round hole into a solid piece of wood and cut lead to fit it, instead of the usual way of gluing the wood in two halves around the filling. Retail price? Twenty-five cents a pencil.

Of course, a superior pencil meant bigger sales. To increase the family income, the Thoreaus also manufactured stove polish,

John Thoreau purchased this Concord house (above) for $1,450 in 1849. The upper story of the ell projection housed his pencil business. Henry Thoreau lived in this house for the last ten years of his life. It was later purchased by Louisa May Alcott, and has since been known as the Thoreau-Alcott house.

Henry Thoreau worked in his father's factory and improved the pencil-making process to the point that Thoreau's Superior Pencil leads became the finest in the United States.

The literary influence of essayist, critic, poet, and philosopher Ralph Waldo Emerson can be found not only in the works of his friend Thoreau, but also in those of Walt Whitman, Emily Dickinson, Herman Melville, and Robert Frost among other American writers.

marbled paper, and sandpaper. But as the pencil sales grew, they dropped everything else. What they didn't realize was that the graphite dust produced in making the pencils was harming Thoreau's lungs, which were already weakened by early tuberculosis.

Certainly the greatest influence on Thoreau during this period was his friendship with Ralph Waldo Emerson (1803–1882). Emerson, thirteen years older than Thoreau, had moved to Concord in 1834, while Thoreau was a student at Harvard. One story holds that they met when Emerson heard that Thoreau had walked twenty miles to hear him lecture.

Emerson had prepared at Harvard for the ministry. But he gave up his pastorate in Boston within three years to travel in Europe, where he became friendly with the notable English writers Thomas Carlyle, Samuel Taylor Coleridge, and William Wordsworth. Their fresh views on philosophy influenced him strongly. When he returned home in 1834, he and his wife settled in Concord, and he began a distinguished career as a writer and lecturer. His oration at Harvard in 1837, "The American Scholar," in which he defined the perfect man, may have been heard by Thoreau.

Emerson's first book, *Nature*, had recently been published. Thoreau had read it in the Harvard library, and it had a profound effect on him. Emerson believed that literature should encourage the study of nature and oneself at the same time. The laws of nature and of human nature were the same. For Emerson, people, regardless of place or time, are essentially the same. There may be differences, but these are far outweighed by the basic sameness of human nature.

In the fall of 1837, a casual acquaintanceship began that would ripen into close friendship. In some ways, Emerson became a substitute father for Thoreau. It was to Emerson that Thoreau looked for guidance. They shared books and the ideas opening out from them. In Emerson's home, Thoreau could meet young and gifted people from all over the country and from abroad too.

Emerson was acknowledged as the leader of the transcendentalist movement. Its central thought, as Thoreau's biographer Walter Harding explains it, is that there is

a body of knowledge innate within man and that this knowledge transcended the senses—thus the name "Transcendentalism." This knowledge was the voice of God within man—his conscience, his moral sense, his inner light,

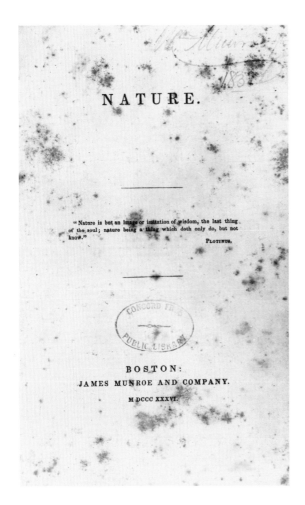

NATURE.

"Nature is but an image or imitation of wisdom, the last thing of the soul; nature being a thing which doth only do, but not know."
PLOTINUS.

BOSTON:
JAMES MUNROE AND COMPANY.
M DCCC XXXVI.

Emerson published this first edition of Nature *anonymously in 1836—thus no author credit on the title page. The groundbreaking book puts forth the foundation of transcendentalism, the movement that was to have such a profound influence on Thoreau.*

his over-soul—and all of these terms and others were used by the various Transcendentalists. But it was central to their belief that the child was born with this innate ability to distinguish between right and wrong. Unfortunately however as he grew older he tended to listen to the world about him rather than the voice within him and his moral sense became calloused. Thus did evil come into the world. And therefore it was the duty, the obligation of the good citizen to return to a childish innocence and heed once more the voice of God within him.

In addition to Walden, *many of Thoreau's natural history writings were set in Walden Woods. Some conservationists look at the Massachusetts site as the birthplace of their movement, as Thoreau did a thorough study of the Walden Woods' ecosystem and called for its preservation.*

Or, as one writer defined it, transcendentalism was "the recognition in man of the capacity of knowing truth instinctively." Many thought Emerson and others who professed this philosophy were vague, dreamy people unable to deal with real issues. But as it turned out, the transcendentalists' idealism would lead them to fight for social and political reform. Their heads were not in the clouds but here on earth, where injustice and inequality summoned them into action to make life better.

In the winter of 1837–1838, while Thoreau was working in the family pencil factory and hoping for a school job, he and Emerson found time for walks out to Walden Pond. Emerson would invite neighbors to come by for an evening of discussion, with Thoreau quick to contribute. "I delight much in my young friend who seems to have as free and erect a mind as any I have ever met," Emerson noted in his journal. "Everything that boy says makes merry with society, though nothing can be graver than his meaning."

Chapter Four

What Can a Man Do?

IT SEEMS LIKELY that it was Emerson who suggested Thoreau keep a journal. And so he did, beginning it on October 22, 1837. It would become the heart of his work. He began it in blank books bought at the local stationer. He used about twenty of these to make notes in and to copy passages from his reading. Another fifty contain over two million words of original writing. Printed long after Thoreau's death, his journal runs to fourteen volumes, with seven thousand pages of text.

The earlier volumes (from 1837 to 1850) are in tatters, for Thoreau cut out many pages to work into the text of what he was writing for publication. Some of the volumes contain snippets of dried plants, sketches, maps, and news clippings. He indexed each volume. Not everything that affected him is found in his journal. But from it, readers can learn much about his life, his ideas, his spirit. It's plain that he worked hard at writing all his life. Yet the problem of earning a living nagged at him. "What may a man do and not be ashamed of it? He may not do nothing, surely," he wrote.

It is a myth that Thoreau didn't care about earning money. He wanted to find not only an audience for his writing but to be paid for it. He would have to deal with editors, publishers, and lyceum managers, and to please them. He could not remain aloof from the literary marketplace.

Here, in passages from his journal, are some of his ideas about writing that any young hopeful may learn from:

> A journal is a record of experiences and growth, not a preserve of things well done or said. I am occasionally reminded of a statement which I have made in conversation and immediately forgotten, which would read much better than what I put in my journal. It is a ripe, dry fruit of long-past experience which falls from me easily, without giving pain or pleasure. The charm of the journal must consist in a certain greenness, though freshness; and not in maturity. Here I cannot afford to be remembering what I said or did, my scurf [scales] cast off, but what I am and aspire to become.

But it was also important "in a few words to describe the weather, or character of the day, as it affects our feelings. That which was so important at the time cannot be unimportant to remember."

He believed, too, in rewriting. His first impressions were usually jotted down rapidly, notes made on the spot, as when he was out in the fields and woods. Later, at home, he expanded these and got a fuller version down in his notebook. In 1857 he explained why two tries at the same thing were often better than one:

> If you are describing any occurrence, or a man, make two or more distinct reports at different times. Though you may think you have said all, you will tomorrow remember a whole new class of facts which perhaps interested most of all at the time, but did not present themselves to be reported. If we have

Thoreau's journals begin on October 22, 1837, with the line, " 'What are you doing now?' he asked, 'Do you keep a journal?' — So I make my first entry to-day." The words are believed to be a response to Ralph Waldo Emerson's inquiry about Thoreau's keeping a journal. Emerson's prod led Thoreau to produce seven-thousand hand-written pages such as this one (right).

recently met and talked with a man, and would report our experience, we commonly make a very partial report at first, failing to seize the most significant, picturesque, and dramatic points; we describe only what we have had time to digest and dispose of in our minds, without being conscious that there were other things really more novel and interesting to us, which will not fail to recur to us and impress us suitably at last.

A few days later, he discussed rewriting again:

I would fain make two reports in my Journal, first the incidents and observations of today; and by tomorrow I review the same and record what was omitted before, which will often be the most significant and poetic part. I do not know at first what it is that charms me. The men and things of today are wont to lie fairer and truer in tomorrow's memory.

"Often," he said, "I can give the truest and most interesting account of any adventure I have had after years have elapsed, for then I am not confused, only the most significant facts surviving in my memory. Indeed, all that continues to interest me after such a lapse of time is sure to be pertinent, and I may safely record all that I remember."

His interest in the particular and the minute is what makes many of his best pages, but there was something more than facts that he wished to set down:

Facts should only be as the frame to my pictures; they should be material to the mythology which I am writing; not facts to assist men to make money, farmers to farm profitably, in any common sense; facts to tell who I am, and where I have been or what I have thought; as now the bell rings for evening meeting, and its volumes of sound, like smoke which rises from where a cannon is fired, to make the tent in which I dwell.

My facts should be falsehoods to the common sense. I would so state facts that they shall be significant, shall be myths or mythologic. Facts which the mind perceived, thoughts which the body thought,—with these I deal. I, too, cherish vague and misty forms, vaguest when the cloud at which I gaze is dissipated quite and naught but the skyey depths are seen.

To speak the truth, Thoreau said, is the one great rule of composition:

Literary gentlemen, editors, and critics think that they know how to write because they have studied grammar and rhetoric;

but the art of composition is as simple as the discharge of a bullet from a rifle, and its masterpieces imply an infinitely greater force behind it. This unlettered man's speaking and writing is standard English. Some words and phrases deemed vulgarisms and Americanisms before, he had made standard American. "It will pay." It suggests that the one great rule of composition—and if I were a professor of rhetoric I should insist on this—is to speak the truth. This first, this second, this third. This demands earnestness and manhood chiefly.

Thoreau had contempt for easy books, but not for simple words:

There are many words, which are genuine and indigenous and have their root in our natures, not made by scholars, and as well understood by the illiterate as others. There are also a great many words which are spurious and artificial, and can only be used in a bad sense, since the thing they signify is not fair and substantial,—such as the church, the judiciary, to impeach, etc., etc. They who use them do not stand on solid ground. It is in vain to try to preserve them by attaching other's words to them as the true church, etc. It is like towing a sinking ship with a canoe.

must have some complicated machinery or other, and hear its din, to
that idea of government which they have. Governments show thus how
cessfully m can

Chapter Five

TEACHING, LOVING, AND BOATING

IN THE FALL OF 1838, Thoreau opened a private school of his own, with his brother John soon joining him. It met first in their own home and later in the deserted building of the old Concord Academy. They set school terms, or quarters, at ten weeks, charging six dollars a term. The school was coeducational. Some students were local. Others, from out of town, boarded with the Thoreau family.

Now Thoreau could set his own rules. No physical punishment, of course. You learned by doing. The brothers adopted new and radical methods of teaching, often anticipating the experiments in education of John Dewey (1859–1952) more than fifty years later.

Thoreau offered languages and science; John taught English and mathematics. They gave informal talks and arranged frequent field trips. One of Thoreau's pupils recalled an example of his teaching methods. One day, out walking with some pupils, Thoreau suddenly stopped, knelt down, and examined the ground with great care. Then, plucking a tiny something, he

Concord Academy.

THE SUBSCRIBER opened his school for the reception of a limited number of pupils, of both sexes, on Monday, September the tenth. Instruction will be given in the usual English branches, and the studies preparatory to a collegiate course.

Terms—Six dollars per quarter.

HENRY D. THOREAU, *Instructor.*

Referees. 〈 Hon. SAM'L HOAR.
Hon. NATHAN BROOKS.
Hon. JOHN KEYES.
Rev. R. W. EMERSON.

Concord, September, 14, 1838.   [45]

An announcement in the September 14, 1838, issue of
Yeoman's Gazette *indicates that Instructor Henry D.*
Thoreau will offer college preparatory classes to a limited
number of pupils of both sexes—for six dollars per quarter!

asked the boy if he could see it. Yes, the boy replied—but what about it? Taking out his magnifying glass, Thoreau showed the boy that thus magnified, this little thing was a perfect flower, just then in its season of blossoming. He went on to say that he had become so well acquainted with the flowers of Concord, large and small, that he could tell what month it was just by the blooming of the flowers.

Thoreau was not trying to display his own superior knowledge. He wanted only to impress on the young mind how immense is the sum of nature's activities, and to help others develop their own sensitivity in such matters.

One of Thoreau's ways of extending his pupils' experience was to take them not only to the fields and woods and ponds but also to visit the shops of local craftsmen. Edmund Sewall, age twelve, in his letters home describes spending time at the local newspaper, watching the compositor setting type, and then at the gunsmith's, where he saw how the gunsmith regulated the sights of a new rifle.

Another time, Thoreau organized a survey of Fairhaven Hill in Concord, and the river shore below it, to give the boys an idea of the fieldwork and instruments of surveying.

In one letter home, Edmund tells his father what they are studying. In the morning, it's geometry, geography, and grammar. In the afternoon, algebra and Latin, and for geography they draw maps of the states. Saturday mornings are given to writing compositions, with Edmund trying his skill describing birds and berries.

The original Concord Academy building in which Henry and John Thoreau established their school in 1838 still stands on Middle Street in Concord, Massachusetts.

School hours were 8:30 to 12:30 and 2:00 to 4:00. Sometimes the school program ran into the evening, as when the pupils were taken to the lyceum to hear a speaker. One lecturer showed them the skull of a British soldier shot in the Battle of Concord. They saw the hole in the skull made by the bullet that killed him. But best of all for Edmund were the Saturday-afternoon field trips the Thoreau brothers took their students on:

> In the afternoon we went off into the woods with a parcel of the boys of the school where we played awhile and drank out [sic] a jug of lemonade we had carried with us. We then left the jug till we came back and started for Walden pond. As we were coming back we saw Aunt and Mr. Thoreau, and I went and joined her while the rest of the boys kept on. We went to Goose pond where we heard a tremendous chirping of frogs. It has been disputed whether the noise was caused by frogs so we were very curious to know what it was. Mr. Thoreau however caught three very small frogs, two of them in the act of chirping. While bringing them home one of them chirped in his hat. He carried them to Mr. Emerson in a tumbler of water. They chirped there also. On Sunday morning I believe he put them in a barrel with some rain water in it. He threw in some sticks for them to rest on. They sometimes crawled up the side of the barrel. I saw one of them chirping. He had swelled out the loose skin of his throat like a little bladder.

The school's reputation was so high that most of the time there was a waiting list of students who wished to enroll. Still, Horace Hosmer recalled that at the end of his first term, John Thoreau told him, "If your father doesn't feel able to send you the next term, you come and you shall have your tuition free."

Thoreau's morning talks, another student said, "showed that he knew himself that to teach broadly and to awaken thought— not merely to hear lessons is the rudiments of letters."

Sadly, brother John's health faded, and he became so ill he could not continue teaching. Thoreau, unwilling to carry the burden alone, closed the school in 1841.

Thoreau fell in love at least once. He lost his heart to Ellen Sewall, the sister of his pupil Edmund Sewall. In July 1839, when Ellen was seventeen and Thoreau was twenty-three, she visited Concord, staying with the Thoreau family for two weeks. Both Henry and John were charmed by the beautiful girl. She went walking and boating with the brothers, and by the time she left, they were both in love with her. In his journal, Henry wrote, "There is no remedy for love but to love more."

Over the next several months John and Ellen exchanged letters, and he sent her presents too. From Henry, nothing. He was unable to speak his heart to her. Besides, he may have felt it was wrong to compete against his older brother. The next summer, Ellen returned to Concord for a visit and went rowing with Henry. He still said nothing of his love for her.

John went again to see Ellen at her home in Scituate, Massachusetts, and this time proposed to her. It startled her, confused her, and without much experience of courtship, she accepted his offer. But giving herself time to think it over, she decided she was more in love with Henry than with John. She told John she had changed her mind.

With John rejected, there was hope for Henry. In November 1840, Henry finally proposed to Ellen in a passionate letter. Ellen, before replying to Henry, told her father. Mr. Sewall, a minister, had strong doubts about both brothers, said to have radical transcendentalist views. He was very much against the marriage, he told her. Ellen wrote Henry that she couldn't marry him.

A few years later, Ellen married a young minister, Joseph Osgood. Thoreau would never marry. When he was dying, he told his sister, "I have always loved Ellen."

In the late summer of 1839, a few weeks after Ellen's first

visit, Henry and John decided it was time for them to enjoy a vacation from teaching. For an excursion to the White Mountains of New Hampshire, they built a rowboat, equipped it with a sail and provisions, and set off on Saturday, August 31. Down the Concord River they went, then up the Merrimack River to the foothills of the White Mountains. Nights, they lay on a buffalo skin under a cotton tent.

On Thursday, September 5, they reached Hooksett, New Hampshire, stored their boat and gear with a friendly farmer, and by stagecoach and on foot reached the mountains. They climbed to the top of Mount Washington, then worked their way back to their boat, returning home on September 13.

This two-week vacation became so important in Thoreau's mind that he made his account of it the basis of his first book, *A Week on the Concord and Merrimack Rivers*. He had kept a journal on the way, and expanding it with essays and poems on many varied subjects—Chaucer, Hindus, friendship, and religion—he enlarged the tale of a rowboat journey into a personal epic. The book would not be published until 1849—ten years later.

But how was Thoreau keeping up with his writing all this time? In his journal, of course. We've seen its beginnings. And before this, in his college days, essays as well as a few poems. The first time his writing reached the public was his lecture on "Society" given at the Concord Lyceum in 1838. It foreshadowed his views of himself as a prophet struggling to find his own voice and an audience to hear it.

When Emerson and other transcendentalists developed plans for a new magazine as an outlet for their ideas, Thoreau made notes for essays he could contribute. The first issue of the *Dial*, edited by Margaret Fuller, appeared in 1840. In it was Thoreau's poem "Sympathy" and an essay on satire. Emerson thought Thoreau's writing was "fresh" and "original." Some readers of the *Dial*, however, found it poor stuff.

An ardent feminist well ahead of her time, Margaret Fuller wrote Woman in the Nineteenth Century *in 1845. The book dealt with feminism in all of its aspects. She also offered lectures to Boston society women on various topics, as well as being the editor of the transcendentalist magazine, the* Dial.

Over the next two years, Fuller rejected all of Thoreau's essays and ran only a few of his poems. Emerson, however, had faith in his protégé. He said, "Thoreau is a scholar and a poet and as full of buds of promise as a young apple tree."

When Emerson took over the editing job himself, he printed Thoreau's essay "The Natural History of Massachusetts." It was

Thoreau's selection of the best nature writing from his journal. Later issues contained several of his poems (not very good) and a few more essays.

The best piece Thoreau wrote for the *Dial* appeared in its final issue, in April 1844. It was his tribute to Nathaniel P. Rogers, the editor of *Herald of Freedom*, the antislavery weekly published in Concord, New Hampshire. Rogers believed that the fight to abolish slavery should be carried on by individuals, not by organizations. Institutions, he thought, interfere with the exercise of freedom by individual abolitionists. Thoreau

Nathaniel Peabody Rogers's Herald of Freedom *newspaper not only spoke out against slavery, but it also defended women's rights. (Engraving from an original painting by H. B. Brown, 1839)*

approved of his antislavery campaigning, and Rogers was deeply grateful to him.

The *Dial* folded with that sixteenth issue, never reaching more than a thousand readers and having only some three hundred subscribers. Yet for Thoreau and others it was the first chance to see their work in print. It proved that what Thoreau had to say, others were willing to print and to read. Now he would try to work his way into publications with broader reach.

In April 1841, after the Thoreau brothers closed their school, Henry was invited to live with the Emersons. He would serve them as handyman and laborer in exchange for room and board. Emerson's son Edward wrote later that Thoreau did all sorts of odd jobs at home and for other people. He also built fences for neighbors that lasted for generations. For Emerson he planted pines in a barren pasture.

The friendship with Emerson intensified when Thoreau's brother, John, and Emerson's little son Waldo died—within two weeks of each other. While shaving on New Year's Day of 1842, John nicked his finger. The mild pain gradually grew worse, and one night lockjaw set in. Lockjaw, or tetanus, is caused by a bacterial infection entering the body through a wound. Stiffness of the jaw is the most common symptom. The doctor said nothing could be done. Thoreau took over care of his brother, who wavered between delirium and calm acceptance of death. John died on January 11, in his brother's arms. At first the family thought Thoreau was strangely calm over their loss. He would sit outdoors and speak to no one. And then, to everyone's shock, on January 22, he too became sick, showing all the symptoms of John's lockjaw but with no sign of a cut. A friend said it was as though a part of him had been torn away.

What was it? The doctor had no answer. The family feared that Thoreau would die too. Then two days later, he began to drift slowly back to normal. But he remained depressed for months

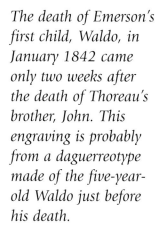

The death of Emerson's first child, Waldo, in January 1842 came only two weeks after the death of Thoreau's brother, John. This engraving is probably from a daguerreotype made of the five-year-old Waldo just before his death.

and was beset by tragic dreams on the anniversary of John's death each year. It must have been what doctors would later call a psychosomatic illness, brought on by his intense, loving connection to his brother.

Only two weeks after John's death, tragedy struck the Emersons. Their five-year-old boy came down with scarlet fever and died three days later. Thoreau had come to love the boy in his months in the Emerson home. Their mutual grief tightened the bonds between Emerson and Thoreau, and Thoreau returned to live in their home.

He had the run of the house again. Edith and Edward, the other Emerson children, thought of him as a kind of older brother. He took them on nature walks and camping trips. By the fireside, he told them stories of his childhood or, more often, of squirrels, muskrats, hawks, the duel of mud turtles in the river, or the great Homeric battle of the red and black ants. He would make their pencils and knives disappear and find them in their ears and noses. And finally, he would get down the heavy copper warming pan from the garret and pop corn for them.

Chapter Six

A Singular Character

IN THE SUMMER OF 1842, Thoreau found a new friend. Nathaniel Hawthorne (1804–1864) and his wife, Sophia Peabody, moved to Concord, Massachusetts. They had rented the Old Manse, an Emerson property, and were happily surprised to find that Thoreau had planted a new garden for them. Hawthorne and Emerson dropped by for a welcoming visit.

Hawthorne, about Emerson's age, was already established in the literary world as the author of many highly praised tales. Stories he would write while in Concord appear in the volume called *Mosses from an Old Manse*. (His later, most distinguished work—*The Scarlet Letter* and *The House of the Seven Gables*—would not be published until 1850 and 1851.)

Friendship between Hawthorne and Thoreau sprang up quickly. Thoreau sold his rowboat to Hawthorne for seven dollars and taught him how to manage it. While they rowed along the Concord River, Hawthorne wrote in his notebook that he found a singular character. . . . He is as ugly as sin, long-nosed, queer-mouthed, and with uncouth and somewhat rustic, although courteous manners, corresponding very well with such an exterior. But his ugliness is of an honest and agreeable fashion, and becomes him much better than beauty. Mr. Thoreau is a keen and delicate observer of nature—a genuine observer, which I suspect, is almost as rare a character as even an original poet; and Nature, in return for his love, seems to adopt him as her especial child, and shows him secrets which few others are allowed to witness. He is familiar with beast, fish, fowl, and reptile, and has strange stories to tell of adventures, and friendly passages with these lower brethren of mortality. Herb and flower, likewise, wherever they grow, whether in garden, or wild wood, are his familiar friends. He is also on intimate terms with the clouds, and can tell the portents of storms. It is a characteristic trait, that he has a great regard for the memory of the Indian tribes, whose wild life would have suited him so well; and strange to say, he seldom walks over a ploughed field without picking up an arrow-point, a spear-head, or other relic of the red men—as if their spirits willed him to be the inheritor of their simple wealth.

When winter iced the river, the three friends—Thoreau, Hawthorne, and Emerson—went skating. Hawthorne liked Thoreau not only as a companion but as a writer. He read Thoreau's natural history essay in the *Dial* and admired it so much he recommended him to the editor of *Sargent's New Monthly Magazine*. "He writes very well indeed," Hawthorne said, "and would be a very valuable contributor."

The *Dial* piece excited the interest of Horace Greeley, editor of the *New York Daily Tribune*. He told his readers that Thoreau wrote

Nathaniel Hawthorne was destined to become one of America's literary greats. He admired his friend and neighbor Henry Thoreau and recommended Thoreau's work to his contacts in publishing.

"in the spirit of the poetic philosopher." The high quality standard Thoreau set would make natural history a popular theme for editors and readers. The *Atlantic Monthly*, among the best publications, would carry his later essays to a far broader audience.

But now, nearing the end of his two-year stay with the Emersons, Thoreau thought he needed to do more to earn some money. The years with the Emersons were a time of growth for Thoreau. He treasured the affection of Emerson, his wife, Lydia, and their children. Helping with production of the *Dial*, he had learned much about the practical side of writing and publishing. His lecturing taught him how to shape his essays for a live audience. Now, at twenty-six, he believed he was ready to make literature his profession.

Emerson, always ready to help, arranged for Thoreau to tutor Willie, then seven, a son of Emerson's brother, William Emerson.

In exchange for board, a room for himself to work in, and one hundred dollars a year, Thoreau agreed to be the "friend and educator" of William Jr., "a boy not yet subdued by schoolmaster," as Emerson put it.

Early in May 1843, Thoreau left Concord for Staten Island, where the William Emersons lived. The island sits in New York Bay, five miles from Manhattan. On its opposite side is the New Jersey shore. Ferryboats carried passengers to and from Manhattan. Pear-shaped, Staten Island is about fourteen miles long and seven miles wide. In that time, it was mostly made up of rural residences, with small communities of middle-class homes.

Thoreau had more in mind than tutoring for small pay. With Manhattan just across the bay, he hoped to connect with editors

Staten Island was a quiet, rural community in the mid-1800s. This view looks at the Narrows, separating Staten Island on the left from Manhattan on the right. Thoreau lived in Judge Emerson's house on Staten Island in 1843.

who might publish, and pay for, his writings. New York, with its three hundred thousand people, was three times the size of Boston. Manhattan was solidly built from its southern tip at the Battery to 15th Street, and streets were laid out for future expansion to 149th Street.

Thoreau tutored Willie each day from nine to two, finding that his even younger brothers, Charles and Haven, quickly joined in. Soon a little friend from across the street began dropping in regularly, making it a full class. Thoreau took the children on long walks and fishing in the bay.

In his off-hours, Thoreau set about exploring the island. He wrote his family a long letter full of his observations of the local flora and fauna, so different from Concord's. "The whole island is like a garden," he said, and ships were always in sight, bound to and from all parts of the world.

Judge William Emerson, elder brother of Ralph Waldo, hired Thoreau to tutor his son Willie in their house on Staten Island, called The Snuggery.

Setting out to explore New York, he was disappointed in what he found. He had not seen the city since the pencil-peddling expedition with his father six years before. "I don't like the city better, the more I see it, but worse. . . . It is a thousand times meaner than I could have imagined. . . . The pigs in the street are the most respectable part of the population. When will the world learn that a million men are of no importance compared with one man?"

But thanks to Emerson's letters of introduction, Thoreau met several people who interested him. Among them were people close to Thoreau's age who favored socialism as the cure for the

As editor of the New York Daily Tribune, *abolitionist Horace Greeley was a champion of the common man. He spoke out in opposition to monopolies, the massive accumulation of wealth in the hands of a few, and land speculation. This 1850 photograph of Greeley was taken by Mathew Brady, who would later achieve fame for his poignant photographs of the Civil War (1861–1865)*

world's troubles. Some were creating socialist communes to prove the value of their ideas. The most important was Horace Greeley, editor of the *New York Daily Tribune*, which he had founded two years earlier. Greeley, then thirty-three, was an ardent abolitionist. Although tremendously busy, he took the time and trouble to offer his services as Thoreau's literary agent.

Greeley knew many influential people in the publishing business and would manage to place some of Thoreau's essays in the leading periodicals. He then plugged the pieces in his own *Tribune*, and he even collected Thoreau's pay for them.

Although Thoreau visited the offices of several publishers, such as *Harper's*, he learned they weren't much interested in publishing his work. No writer, and especially a new and young one, could expect to make a living by his pen. Even the popular poet Longfellow lamented that "nobody pays nowadays." Magazines at that time did not sell space to advertisers. They relied solely on money derived from sales of the publication. Those with large readership were often in trouble because subscribers weren't paying up. The contents of the weekly papers were made up mostly of reprinted material. There was no international copyright law, and it cost the publishers nothing to "borrow" material from English or foreign publications. Book publishers, too, were freely reprinting foreign books on which they paid no royalties. It was an age of piracy. The oversize weekly newspapers took to reprinting as "supplements" cheap editions of novels they had previously pirated and run in serial form. It got so bad that a thieving weekly paper hired a thug to break into *Harper's* bindery and steal a new popular novel. He then set the building on fire to destroy the bindery.

Thoreau wrote his family that on Staten Island he had met only one man he'd like to know better, "an old fisherman who invites me to come to the beach where he spends the week and see him and his fish. . . . Farms are for sale all around here—and so I suppose men are for purchase."

The Train Whistle Blows

While Thoreau was in Staten Island, Concord, Massachusetts, was changing rapidly. The swift advance of technology was forcing eighteenth-century New England into the industrial age. America had already seen one of its first railroads in 1826. It ran from the granite quarries of Quincy, Massachusetts, to the Neponset River three miles away. A Boston and Fitchburg line would pass through Concord, and the town became full of Irish immigrants working on its construction. The work was done by manual labor, with the mainly Irish workers earning fifty to sixty cents for a sixteen-hour day.

Thoreau thought this was slave-driving. But what could be done when men seeking work were pouring in every day? The competition for jobs kept wages down. No man could support a family on such low pay.

If you boarded the train for Boston, it cost you fifty cents for the one-hour ride. It was one-third cheaper than taking the stage-coach, and it took only one hour, not four. Both Thoreau and Emerson feared the noisy new contraption would change everything. Emerson thought briefly of moving out of Concord. But neither man could have guessed that the railroad would play a decisive role in nearly every major movement in American history.

Emerson wrote to Thoreau that Concord was full of Irish, and the woods with engineers and their red flags, staking out the route on the new Fitchburg Railroad from station to station. Thoreau reported that he had placed only a book review and an essay in the *Democratic Review* and that one paper had taken his piece "A Walk to Wachusett." To his mother he wrote, "I hold together remarkably well as yet, speaking of my outward linen and woolen man, no holes more than I brought away, and no stitches needed yet. It is marvellous." And he had bought some ready-made pantaloons, costing $2.25.

Standing on one of Staten Island's hills, overlooking the bay, Thoreau wrote he could

observe one aspect of the modern world at least—I mean the migratory—the western movement. Sixteen hundred immigrants arrived at quarantine ground on the fourth of July, and more or less every day since I have been here. I see them occasionally washing their persons and clothes, or men, women and children gathered on an isolated quay near the shore, stretching their limbs and taking the air, the children running races and swinging—on their artificial piece of the land of liberty—while the vessels are undergoing purification. They are detained but a day or two, and then go up to the city, for the most part without having landed here. I have crossed the bay 20 or 30 times and have seen a great many immigrants going up to the city for the first time—Norwegians who carry their old fashioned farming tools to the west with them, and will buy nothing here for fear of being cheated.—English operatives, known by their pale faces and stained hands, who will recover their birth-rights in a little cheap sun and wind,—English travellers on their way to the Astor House, to whom I have done the honors of the city.—Whole families of immigrants cooking their dinner upon the pavements, all sunburnt—so that you are in doubt where the foreigner's face of flesh begins—their tidy clothes laid on, and then tied to their swathed bodies which move about like a bandaged finger—caps set on the head, as if woven of the hair, which is still growing at the roots—each and all busily cooking, stooping from time to time over the pot, and having something to drop into it, that so they may be entitled to take something out, forsooth. They look like respectable but straightened [sic] people, who may turn out to be counts when they get to Wisconsin— and will have their experience to relate to their children.

Thoreau went home for the Thanksgiving holiday, delivering a lecture on the "Ancient Poets" before the Concord Lyceum. Then, too homesick to remain on Staten Island, he returned to pack his things, and in December bid good-bye to his little class. Never again would he live away from Concord.

Chapter Seven

BUILDING
A HOUSE—
AND A BOOK

BACK WITH HIS FAMILY IN CONCORD, Thoreau once again went to work in his father's pencil factory. He needed to earn enough to pay off his debts. He set out to develop the methods and machines to make Thoreau pencils the best in the business. They were so superior that art teachers insisted their students buy only Thoreau pencils.

The fine weather of late April 1844 led Thoreau to take off a few days to row up the Sudbury River. He took along young Edward Hoar, son of Concord's leading citizen, Samuel Hoar. A Harvard senior, Edward had sometimes joined Thoreau in wandering through the woods. This day they went ashore at Fairhaven Bay to cook a luncheon of fish they had just caught. With the ground quite dry, a stray spark from their fire set the dead grass aflame. They tried frantically to stamp it out, but the fire raced swiftly uphill. Unable to halt its spread, Thoreau and Hoar ran for help. Too late. The flames were raging. As alarm bells rang in the village, crowds rushed to the scene to put out the fire.

More than three hundred acres were burned, at a cost to the three landowners of two thousand dollars in damage. Thoreau and Hoar were accused of being thoughtless and careless. Some wanted to prosecute the two men, but Hoar's family standing saved them from that. His father apparently paid damages to the landowners. Some of the angry townsfolk for years afterwards would speak of Thoreau as that "woods-burner."

Fire in the Woods.—A fire broke out in the woods near Fairhaven Pond, in this town, about ten o'clock, last Tuesday forenoon. It extended with great rapidity, and was not subdued until late in the afternoon. The extent of ground over which the fire prevailed, is variously estimated, the lowest estimate placing it at not less than 300 acres. The damage is estimated at about $2000, and falls principally upon Mr A. H. Wheeler, Mr Cyrus Hubbard, and Mr Darius Hubbard. Several other persons have lost something by the disaster, but not so largely as the gentlemen named. Mr Wheeler had some sixty cords of wood which had been cut and piled, destroyed. Our citizens turned out very generally, and labored with great zeal and efficiency to stay the progress of the fire. Their labors were crowned with all the success that could have been expected, when we consider the exceeding dryness of the woods, —there having been no rain of consequence for weeks, —and the difficulties against which they had to contend. By trenching, beating the fire with pine branches, and lighting 'back fires,' all of which was done coolly and systematically, a large quantity of property was saved, and the fire prevented from spreading. The fire at times made a very magnificent appearance, but as it was mainly confined to the young wood, underbrush, and leaves, it could not have been seen at any very great distance. Dense clouds of smoke rose at times, and gave the impression that the fire was more destructive than it really was. We were forcibly reminded of the scene in Cooper's 'Pioneers,' in which a burning forest is so graphically described.

The fire, we understand, was communicated to the woods through the thoughtlessness of two of our citizens, who kindled it in a *pine stump*, near the Pond,

The news article in the May 3, 1844 Concord Freeman reported that a fire was "communicated to the woods through the thoughtlessness of two of our citizens . . ." an "unfortunate result of sheer carelessness."

Transcendentalist poet Ellery Channing was a good friend to Emerson, Alcott, Hawthorne, and especially Thoreau. Channing is remembered less for his poetry, which Thoreau once characterized as "sublime slipshod," than for his 1873 biography of his friend, Thoreau, the Poet-Naturalist.

In May, Thoreau and his friend Ellery Channing went on a mountain climbing excursion. Channing, a Harvard dropout, had met Thoreau at the Emersons' in 1840. A few years later, Ellery married Margaret Fuller's sister Ellen, and they rented a house in Concord, which Thoreau had found for them. Thoreau did all sorts of repairs and improvements for them before they moved in. Channing had been unhappy when Thoreau left Concord for Staten Island.

Back at home in Concord, Thoreau renewed his friendship with Channing. However, it soon would be Channing's turn to move away from Concord. He took a job with Greeley's *Tribune* and moved to New York. On one occasion, Thoreau hiked across the state to meet Channing at Pittsfield in the Berkshires. From there they traveled west to the Hudson River and boated down to the Catskills, where they hiked into the mountains.

People who knew them considered both men rather odd and unpredictable. They were staunch individualists yet became the closest of friends. Walter Harding, Thoreau's biographer, believed theirs was "the most intimate and lasting friendship of Thoreau's life."

Channing, some ten years after Thoreau's death, wrote the first biography of his friend. In it he describes Thoreau memorably:

> In height, [Thoreau] was about the average, in his build, spare, with limbs that were rather longer than usual, or of which he made a longer use. His face, once seen, could not be forgotten. The features were quite marked: the nose aquiline or very Roman, like one of the portraits of Caesar (more like a beak, as was said); large, overhanging brows above the deepest set blue eyes that could be seen, in certain lights, and in others gray,—eyes expressive of all shades of feeling, but never weak or near-sighted; the forehead not unusually broad or high, full of concentrated energy and purpose; the mouth with prominent lips, pursed up with meaning and thought when silent, and giving out when open a stream of the most varied and unusual instructive sayings. His hair was a dark brown, exceedingly abundant, fine and soft. . . . His whole figure had an active earnestness, as if he had no moment to waste. The clenched hand betokened purpose. In walking, he made a short cut if he could, and when sitting in the shade or by the wallside seemed merely the clearer to look forward into the next piece of activity. Even in the boat he had a wary, transitory air, his eyes on the outlook,—perhaps there might be ducks, or the Blondin turtle, or an otter, or sparrow.

Thoreau returned from his trip with Channing just before Emerson came out publicly for the freeing of America's slaves. August 1, 1844, marked the tenth anniversary of the law in Great Britain that had abolished slavery in all its territories. Prodded by Thoreau's mother and her circle of abolitionist women, Emerson agreed to speak on emancipation in the British West Indies. (Of course Thoreau was there, sitting among the antislavery women of thirteen towns, all of whom were thrilled that so admired a public figure as Emerson had joined their cause.)

Antislavery Movement

The movement to abolish slavery was not supported by the conservative people of Concord. Thoreau's energetic mother had become an activist in that cause and gathered other women to support it. When Emerson spoke for abolition in August 1844, it was Thoreau who rang the church bell to gather a crowd to hear the speech. And it was Thoreau again who arranged for a Boston publisher to print it in pamphlet form.

Wendell Phillips

Earlier, in December 1842, Thoreau had invited Wendell Phillips, the country's leading abolitionist orator, to speak at the Concord Lyceum. His frank exposé of Northern complicity in profiting from slavery had enraged the town's leaders. Asked to speak a year later, Phillips again gave a speech that angered the conservatives. When a third invitation to the abolitionist was proposed, the curators of the lyceum resigned in protest and were replaced by Emerson and Thoreau. Phillips spoke on March 11, 1845, and the next day, Thoreau wrote to William Lloyd Garrison's paper, the *Liberator*, a long letter focusing on the event as a triumph for freedom of speech.

The abolition movement never won mass support before the Civil War. Concord was but one town of many where the crucial issue caused angry debate and sometimes mob violence.

Yet there were enough abolitionists in Concord to make it a station on the Underground Railroad. In *Walden* Thoreau notes that among the visitors beside the pond was a runaway slave he helped to forward to Canada.

Thoreau's father rented a number of houses before he could accumulate the funds to build a home of his own. This house, built in 1844, was on Texas Street, which became Belknap Street, in Concord.

Emerson's was a powerful, richly detailed speech on the progressive development of the British antislavery movement to the point of complete emancipation. What was wrong with the American democracy that it could not see its way to doing the same? Emerson cleverly designed it not to pat the minority of abolitionists on the back, but to convince the great majority of others of what they needed to do to free America's slaves.

That September, with the pencil business doing so well, Thoreau's father bought a vacant lot on what was then Texas Street and later became is Belknap Street. Mrs. Thoreau chose the site and drew up the plans. Thoreau and his father worked together to build the house. It would be their first family-owned home. All the others had been rented. It took a lot of Thoreau's time, but he was learning something new and valuable.

Building a house was a great construction challenge. So was building a first book. And that fall, Thoreau began to do just that.

Chapter Eight

A CABIN ON WALDEN POND

THOREAU HAD LONG been interested in living the simple life. In the last paper he wrote at Harvard, he advocated reversing the biblical formula; he was for working one day a week and resting six. Vacations spent in a classmate's cabin on Flint's Pond while still in college increased Thoreau's desire to live in a secluded setting.

There were many others who dreamed of living a life removed from the intense pressures of a competitive society, where the goal was to get rich quick. By now the first utopian communities, such as Brook Farm, had been founded, forerunners of many others that would soon spring up.

In the fall of 1844, the chance to have his own place in the wild opened up. Emerson had just bought land on the shore of Walden Pond, a beautiful glacial lake of about sixty-one acres, less than two miles from Concord village.

Thoreau asked Emerson if, in return for clearing some of the scrubland and reforesting it with pines, he could build a cabin

Josiah Walcott painted this view of Brook Farm in 1844. Hawthorne lived at the farm from April to November of 1841.

and live there rent-free. For Thoreau, who enjoyed relying on his own energy and skills, life at Walden would be his personal path to freedom.

It wasn't just that Thoreau wanted to escape from the busy world. He believed living a simple life would give him the freedom to devote himself to writing. To be a professional writer was his goal. But how could he devote himself to it if he had to keep scrambling to make a living? By doing away with the pressure to make money, he could write what he wished, the way he wished.

Thoreau knew what he wanted to write. It would be a book about the rowboat journey on the Concord and Merrimack rivers into New Hampshire and back that he and his brother John had taken in 1839. He had cherished the idea of the book as a memorial to his brother ever since John's tragic death in 1842. He meant the book to be an elegy, a poem.

With Emerson's permission, in late March 1845, Thoreau went to Walden Pond and, with a borrowed axe, began to cut down the pines for the wood he needed to build his cabin. By mid-April the cabin was framed, ready for raising. He placed it about two hundred feet up a gentle slope from the shore of a cove. It wasn't an isolated spot. The road between the villages of Concord and Lincoln was in sight, and on the opposite end of the pond, trains traversing the Boston–Fitchburg Railroad chugged by.

It took another two months for Thoreau to complete the carpentry. With the arrival of warm weather, he cleared a briar field

Thoreau chose to locate his new home near Walden Pond (above). *The location had been one of Thoreau's favorite places since boyhood.*

Thoreau lived in the Walden Pond cabin of his own making for two years and two months. What became of it after he left it is a mystery, although it was believed to have been moved several times. In November 1945, a Thoreau enthusiast visiting Walden Pond unearthed the hearth of the original building. Researchers later worked with the state to reconstruct the cabin (above) *from Thoreau's written descriptions and drawings.*

and planted two and a half acres. His beans and potatoes he would sell; the corn, peas, and turnips he'd eat himself.

His new nest was ten feet wide and fifteen feet long. It had a garret, closet, windows on each side, an entry door, and a brick fireplace opposite. In back was a woodshed and an outhouse. The pond was his bathtub and refrigerator. A nearby spring provided clean drinking water.

Thoreau added up his building costs. They came to $28.12. His friend Ellery Channing, who dropped in often, called the cabin a wooden inkstand, convenient for shelter, sleep, or meditation. When Channing stayed overnight, he slept on the floor beneath Thoreau's slatted bed. The furniture was mostly homemade—a table, desk, three chairs, and a bed. Thoreau also had eating and cooking utensils.

After eight months in the cabin, Thoreau tallied the cost of his food: $8.74, clothing: $8.40, and fuel: $2.00. You had to admit that as an economic experiment, it worked well. True, his mother and sisters trotted out every Saturday with dishes they had cooked. And the Emersons and other friends often had him in for dinner.

No, contrary to popular legend, Thoreau wasn't living like a hermit at the pond. Hardly a day passed that he did not visit his friends and relatives in the village or that they didn't come out to the pond to see him.

When he was alone at the pond, he did his housecleaning early in the morning, and then he might do some gardening. On some summer days, he might just sit in his doorway, thinking, dreaming, loafing in the sun. In colder weather, he took on paying jobs as fence builder, painter, gardener, carpenter. For one man he built a fireplace, and for another, a woodshed. He also tackled surveying. It took him out of doors, paid decently, and was satisfying work.

Mornings in Thoreau's small house were often spent writing at his desk. Afternoons, he walked in the woods and fields or rowed on the rivers and ponds. In the evening, he might row out on the pond and play his flute or fish. He did close studies of how the changing seasons affected pond life and made surveys of its size and depth. In the winter of 1846–1847, he watched an ice merchant's crew of a hundred Irish workmen harvest tons of ice for shipment to warmer places such as New Orleans and India. That led him to study the temperature of Walden and to compare it with that of nearby ponds, rivers, and springs. Such statistical studies became almost a mania for him. His findings recorded in the journal would amaze scientists with their accuracy.

Emerson visited him often and hired him to do odd jobs from surveying to gardening, noting, "Henry is so thoughtful and does so much more than is bargained for. When he does anything I am sure the thing is done." But not all was work; there was fun too, with Thoreau picnicking or blueberry picking with the Emerson family.

Calling on all his skills, Thoreau found he could support himself by working no more than a total of six weeks a year. He wrote Horace Greeley, "I am convinced, both by faith and experience, that to maintain one's self on this earth is not a hardship but a pastime, if we will live simply and wisely. . . . It is not necessary that a man should earn his living by the sweat of his brow, unless he sweats easier than I do."

But what about his writing? Thoreau left himself plenty of free time for it. First he wrote a long essay on Thomas Carlyle, an English author and one of the early transcendentalists. He used the essay for a lecture before the Concord Lyceum early in 1846. Although the listeners liked it, they had expected him to tell why he, a Harvard graduate, had turned his back on a paying career to live in a cabin in the woods. They told Thoreau bluntly that's what they'd hoped to hear.

Thoreau then began working on a series of lectures that would grow into his masterwork, *Walden; or, Life in the Woods*. It took him twelve months to create his first Walden lecture for his townsfolk. On February 2, 1847, he read them his "History of Myself." Later it became the "Economy" chapter of the book. It must have been very good, because the lyceum patrons did something extraordinary: they asked him to repeat it a week later for people who had missed it.

Louisa May Alcott was a child when Thoreau was living at Walden Pond. When she grew up she became the author of famous books such as *Little Women*. He was teacher and older brother to her and her sisters Amy and Beth. Their father, Bronson Alcott, would take the family to see Thoreau at the pond. Thoreau made a strong impression on Louisa, who years later recalled:

> [He] used to come smiling up to his neighbors, to announce that the bluebirds had arrived, with as much interest in the fact as other men take in messages by the Atlantic cable. On certain days, he made long pilgrimages to find "the sweet rhodora in the wood," welcoming the lonely flower like a long-absent friend. He gravely informed us once, that frogs were much more confiding in the spring, than later in the season; for then, it only took an hour to get well acquainted with one of the speckled swimmers, who like to be tickled with a blade of grass, and would feed from his hand in the most sociable manner.

must have some complicated machinery or other, and hear its din, to
that idea of government which they have. Governments show thus ho
cessfully men can even impose on themselves, for the

Chapter Nine

A NIGHT IN JAIL

SETTING TO WORK in his cabin by the pond, Thoreau began his tale of the 1839 vacation voyage with his brother John by greatly expanding his original journal entries. For about half the book, he tells of their boating and camping experiences and describes the scenery along the way. These passages are lyrical in their beauty. Yet *A Week* is more than a travel book. Thoreau planted in it many quotations from his favorite readings and added some of his own poems and essays on varied subjects. These essays run from just a paragraph to several pages and veer off in all directions from the travel narrative. Yet, as Robert Richardson, a Thoreau biographer, points out, "*A Week* has strong, if frequently overlooked, social themes: friendship, settlement, Indian life, oriental law."

On July 12, 1846, Thoreau reached his twenty-ninth birthday. Two weeks later, on his way into Concord from his Walden cabin to pick up a shoe that was being repaired, he was arrested. The charge? Nonpayment of the poll tax, a tax he had not paid for four years.

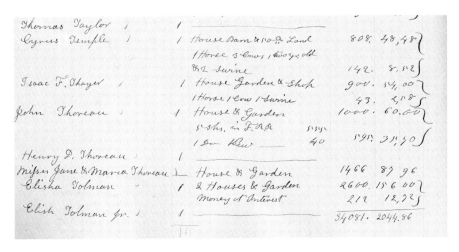

Henry D. Thoreau's name appears just below that of his father on the Concord tax record. John appears to have paid his taxes, while the columns after Henry's name are blank.

His jailer was neighbor Sam Staples. "Henry knew that I had a warrant for him," Staples said, "but I didn't go to hunt for him. I knew I could git [sic] him when I wanted to."

With Thoreau locked up, Sheriff Staples decided to go out and take care of some other business. When he was gone, someone rapped at the door of the sheriff's apartment in the jail. When his little daughter opened the door, a veiled woman said, "Here is the money to pay Mr. Thoreau's tax." She left immediately, without telling who she was.

Word of Thoreau's arrest spread quickly through the town. No one is sure who paid the taxes without his permission. But most believe it was his Aunt Maria Thoreau. Although the tax debt was cleared up, Staples recalled, he had taken his boots off and was sitting by the fire. He didn't feel like taking the trouble to unlock the cell door and let Thoreau out. No, he kept him until after breakfast the next morning. When Staples told Thoreau he was free to go, Staples was astonished to find that his prisoner did not

The character of Thoreau's Aunt Maria shone through in her frequent correspondence, much of which has been preserved. An energetic and intelligent woman, she espoused reform causes and was an abolitionist.

want to leave and was "mad as the devil!" He wanted his refusal to pay taxes to arouse the citizens to protest too. But finally Thoreau went on his way, got his repaired shoe at the cobbler's, and walked back to his cabin.

Thoreau wasn't the first or only man in Concord to refuse to pay his taxes on principle. Three years earlier, Bronson Alcott and Charles Lane had been arrested for nonpayment. It was their dramatic way of demonstrating their detestation of a government that supported slavery.

The significance of Thoreau's act was what his pen did with the experience. It inspired him to write what was to become the most widely read and most influential of all his works. It was the essay the world now knows as "Civil Disobedience."

Two months earlier, on May 13, 1846, the United States had declared war on Mexico. It was a war Thoreau believed to be started by the United States on behalf of slaveholders who wished to extend their slave territory. From the beginning, the abolitionists opposed the war on moral grounds. Some religious groups—the Quakers, the Unitarians, the Congregationalists— also opposed the war. The Reverend William Henry Channing even said that if he had to fight in the "damnable war," it would be on the side of the Mexicans.

Boston minister Theodore Parker preached a sermon to his congregation of seven thousand members in which he answered the great question of the day—what shall we do about this war?—and linked slavery to the issue:

> We can refuse to take any part in it; we can encourage others to do the same; we can aid men, if need be, who suffer because they refuse. Men will call us traitors; what then? That hurt nobody in '76. We are a rebellious nation; our whole history is treason; our constitution treason to our fatherland. What of that? Though all the governors of the world bid us commit treason against man, and set the example, let us never submit. Let God alone be a master to control our conscience.

The war ended on February 2, 1848, with Mexico forced to sign a peace treaty. By the agreement, the United States acquired 850,000 square miles—about one-third of Mexico's land. It was more than the combined area of France, Spain, and Italy. As the treaty was being signed, Horace Greeley wrote in his *New York Daily Tribune*, "Sign anything, ratify anything, pay anything, to end the guilt, the bloodshed, the shame, the enormous waste of this horrible contest."

Meeting Thoreau soon after his jailing, Emerson asked why he'd gone to jail, only to have his young friend reply, "Waldo, why are you not here?"

Many of the townsfolk wanted Thoreau to explain his reason for voluntarily going to jail. To satisfy them, he prepared a lecture on the duty of the individual to the state and read it before the

Concord Lyceum. It aroused such interest that he was asked to read it again a few weeks later.

Elizabeth Peabody, sister-in-law of author Nathaniel Hawthorne, ran a bookshop in Boston and was a friend of many of the city's writers. In the spring of 1848, she told Thoreau she'd like to run his essay in the first issue of her new periodical, *Aesthetic Papers*. She meant her publication to carry on the tradition of the now-defunct *Dial*. Six weeks later the periodical appeared (it would be the only issue), with pieces by Emerson and Hawthorne as well as Thoreau's piece, which was retitled "Resistance to Civil Government."

His essay made little impression at the time. People were drawn more to Emerson and Hawthorne than to this relatively unknown writer.

It was not until 1866 (four years after Thoreau's death), when the essay, again retitled "Civil Disobedience," appeared that its

Among the many accomplishments of Elizabeth Palmer Peabody, sister-in-law of author Nathaniel Hawthorne and educational reformer Horace Mann, was the establishment in 1860 of the first formally organized American kindergarten in Boston.

influence began to spread in wave after wave across the globe. What he had done and what he had to say about its meaning has had a universal appeal. Why? Because it spoke to the issue of moral law in conflict with civil law:

> Government is at best but an expedient; but most governments are sometimes, inexpedient. . . . The government itself, which is only the mode which the people have chosen to execute their will, is . . . liable to be abused and perverted before the people can act through it. Witness the present Mexican War, the work of comparatively a few individuals using the standing government as their tool; for, in the outset, the people would not have consented to this measure. . . . This people must cease to hold slaves, and to make war on Mexico, though it cost them their existence as a people.

He was saying that a law should be respected not because it is a law, but only if it is just and right. If unjust laws exist, civil disobedience, such as refusing to pay taxes, is an effective way to oppose and change them.

Chapter Ten

CIVIL DISOBEDIENCE

THE CONCEPT of nonviolent resistance to evil has deep roots in American history. In the 1700s, before the United States became an independent nation, John Woolman and other Quakers traveled through the South, trying to convince slaveholders that they should give up slavery on moral grounds. Antislavery and antiwar reformers in the 1830s, such as William Lloyd Garrison, spread the same message.

Thoreau's was a radical view of conscientious objection. He held that there's a higher law than the government's law. And that's the law of conscience. When these two laws conflict, it's the citizen's duty to obey the voice of conscience rather than that of the government. By so acting, one may awaken fellow citizens to a wrong and make them willing to correct it.

Thoreau's doctrine of civil disobedience would move people around the world to act peacefully against war and oppression. In India, Mohandas Gandhi (1869–1948) developed satyagraha, a concept that organized nonviolent action into mass moral pressure for achieving social and political goals. Civil disobedience was one of Gandhi's main tools for winning independence for India without bringing about a bloody war between the people of India and the occupying British.

Gandhi's principle of peaceful nonviolent resistance to oppression appealed to African American leaders. With petitions for racial equality getting nowhere, in January 1941, A. Philip Randolph, head of the Brotherhood of Sleeping Car Porters, proposed a March on Washington to demand that the government do something. Alarmed by the signs of mass protest, President Franklin Roosevelt said there was no need to march; he would do what they asked. He quickly issued Executive Order 8802, which banned discrimination in defense industries and government "because of race, creed, color, or national origin," and set up a federal agency to carry out the order. At last, some eighty years

Many people consider Thoreau the father of civil disobedience, a peaceful political strategy that Mohandas Ghandi later applied to the movement for the independence of India from Great Britain.

after Lincoln's Emancipation Proclamation, a president had acted to protect the rights of African Americans.

It was a good beginning, but much more needed to be done. Soon others were studying Gandhi's nonviolent method, using it as a force for social change. In the Second World War (1939–1945), about fifty thousand conscientious objectors accepted assignment to the armed forces but did only noncombatant duty. Six thousand conscientious objectors went to prison rather than take part in any aspect of the war.

In the 1950s, it was the Reverend Martin Luther King Jr., together with other blacks and whites, who shaped nonviolent resistance to injustice into such powerful protests as bus boycotts, sit-ins, and mass marches. For Dr. King, it wasn't just a strategy effective for the time, but a way of life.

Thoreau's essay inspired not only Gandhi and King, but also the Danish resistance to Nazism, student protests against the Vietnam War, the struggle to end apartheid in South Africa, and the Tiananmen Square uprising for democracy in China.

Civil Disobedience

Here are key passages from Thoreau's essay "Civil Disobedience":

Unjust laws exist: shall we be content to obey them, or shall we endeavor to amend them, and obey them until we have succeeded, or shall we transgress them at once? Men generally, under such a government as this, think that they ought to wait until they have persuaded the majority to alter them. They think that, if they should resist, the remedy would be worse than the evil. But it is the fault of the government itself that the remedy is worse than the evil. It makes it worse. Why is it not more apt to anticipate and provide for reform? Why does it not cherish its wise minority? Why does it cry and resist before it is hurt? Why does it not encourage its citizens to be on the alert to point out its faults, and do better than it would have them? Why does it always crucify Christ, and excommunicate Copernicus and Luther, and pronounce Washington and Franklin rebels? . . .

Under a government which imprisons any unjustly, the true place for a just man is also a prison. The proper place today, the only place which Massachusetts has provided for her freer and less desponding spirits, is in her prisons, to be put out and locked out of the State by her own act, as they have already put themselves out by their principles. It is there that the fugitive slave, and the Mexican prisoner on parole, and the Indian come to plead the wrongs of his race should find them; on that separate, but more free and honorable ground, where the State places those who are not with her, but against her—the only house in a slave State in which a free man can abide with honor. If any think that their influence would be lost there, and their voices no longer afflict the ear of the State, that they would not be as an enemy within its walls, they do not know by how much truth is stronger than error, nor how much more eloquently and effectively he can combat injustice who has experienced a little in his own person. Cast your whole vote, not a strip of paper merely, but your whole influence. A minority is powerless while it conforms to the majority; it is not even a minority then; but it is irresistible when it clogs by its whole weight. If the alternative is to keep all just men in prison, or give up war and slavery, the State will not hesitate which to choose. If a thousand men were not to pay their tax-bills this year, that would not be a violent and bloody measure, as it would be to pay them, and enable the State to commit violence and shed innocent blood. This is, in fact, the definition of a peaceable revolution, if any such is possible. If the tax-gatherer, or any other public officer, asks me, as one has done, "But what shall I do?" my answer is, "If you really wish to do anything, resign your office." When the subject has refused allegiance, and the officer has resigned his office, then the revolution is accomplished. But even suppose blood should flow. Is there not a sort of blood shed when the conscience is wounded? Through this wound a man's real manhood and immortality flow out, and he bleeds to an everlasting death. I see this blood flowing now. . . .

His homemade desk was one of the few pieces of furniture in Thoreau's Walden cabin. It was on this desk that he penned Walden *and "Civil Disobedience."*

Chapter Eleven

SURVEYOR AND LECTURER

WHILE STILL LIVING in his cabin at Walden, Thoreau took on surveying jobs. The first was in the spring of 1847, when he surveyed a lot Emerson had just bought. His pay for the job: one dollar. Thoreau found this work a good way to eke out a living for it didn't take up too much time. His comments on the variety of people he worked for appeared in his journal. Of one of these, Sam Staples, his jailer, Thoreau wrote that he was "quick, clever, downright shy, and on the whole a good fellow, especially good to treat with rougher and slower men than himself, always meaning well."

Concord appointed Thoreau surveyor-in-chief, assigning him to lay out roads, walk the bounds with the town officials, and supply the technical documents for lawsuits involving his craft. He soon knew more about his neighbors' property than they did. Sometimes people in other towns hired him for surveying.

When Thoreau died, he left a sizable body of working papers—field notes and draft surveys. They include a complete

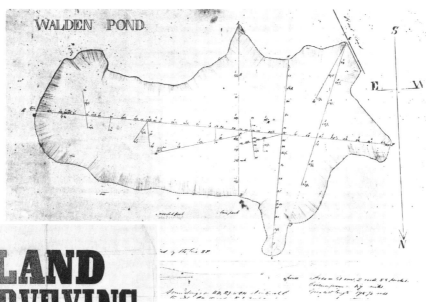

WALDEN POND.

LAND SURVEYING

Of all kinds, according to the best methods known; the necessary data supplied, in order that the boundaries of Farms may be accurately described in Deeds; *Woods* lotted off distinctly and according to a regular plan; *Roads* laid out, &c., &c. Distinct and accurate Plans of Farms furnished, with the buildings thereon, of any size, and with a scale of feet attached, to accompany the Farm Book, so that the land may be laid out in a winter evening.

Areas warranted accurate within almost any degree of exactness, and the Variation of the Compass given, so that the lines can be run again. Apply to

HENRY D. THOREAU,

Thoreau made more than 150 land surveys in and around Concord. Modern surveyors, using far more sophisticated equipment than was available to Thoreau, say that his work was excellent. There have been a number of surveys on the depth of Walden Pond commissioned in modern times, and the results do not disprove Thoreau's conclusions, made only from a string and a stone. The handbill (left) advertises Thoreau's services.

survey of almost every farm in town. About two hundred of these—made between 1849 and 1861—are still held in the Concord Free Public Library.

Lecturing was another means of support for Thoreau. He often talked on such popular topics as natural history, biography, and literature. For his lectures at the Concord Lyceum—he gave nineteen of these—he was paid nothing. He and the other local people donated their services. When a leading light like Emerson spoke out of town, he was paid fifty dollars. But Thoreau's fees were always small.

Thoreau said he wasn't interested in fees. But he knew others were: "Men's minds run so much on work and money that the mass instantly associates literary labor with a pecuniary reward. They are mainly anxious to know how much money the lecturer or author gets for his work." Such people, he added, "never dream of any other use for writing."

He felt he cheapened himself by trying to become a popular lecturer. He thought the public demanded an average man, not originality, not excellence. The more you were like them, the better they liked you. "I'd rather write books than lectures!"

Like Emerson, Thoreau's aim was to reform listeners rather than echo their popular values. Yet his lectures did appeal to many listeners. When he spoke in Portland, Maine, in March 1849, the local paper reported:

CONCORD LYCEUM.

THERE is a Lecture before this Institution every Wednesday Evening, at 7 o'clock precisely. The course for the present season, as far as ascertained, is as follows :

Nov. 18, (Introductory) R. W. Emerson, Concord.
" 30, R. W. Emerson, Concord.
Dec. 7, James Richardson, Cambridge.
" 14, James Freeman Clarke, Boston.
" 19, (Extra lecture) Horace Greeley, N. York.
" 21, Wendell Phillips, Boston.
" 28, O. A. Brownson, Chelsea.
Jan. 4, Charles Lane, England.
Jan. 11, M. B. Prichard, Concord.
" 18, John S. Keyes, Cambridge.
" 25, J. F. Barrett, Boston.
Feb. 1, C. T. Jackson, "
" 8, H. D. Thoreau, Concord.

" 15, E. H. Chapin, Charlestown.
Mar. 16, Henry Giles, England.
" 22, Edward Jarvis, Louisville.
All are invited to attend. By order of the Curators.
January 6, 1843. tf

Thoreau is listed as a speaker on February 8, 1843, at the Concord Lyceum. He lectured on Sir Walter Raleigh.

> The lecture was unique, original, comical and high-falutin. It kept the audience wide awake, and most pleasantly excited for two hours. It was like the dashing out of a comet that had broken loose from its orbit—hitting here and there, a gentle tap at this folly, and a severe one at that—but all in good nature.

It was higher praise than Greeley and Emerson would receive for their lectures in Portland soon after.

Although Thoreau never became a star on the lyceum circuit, his lectures were important to his literary career. The personal interaction with the public helped him to clarify his ideas. As Professor Steven Fink has pointed out, "Lecturing helped Thoreau shape his identity as both a prophet and an artist. The lecture platform served as a testing ground, a place for Thoreau to listen to his own words and to see how an audience responded to them. Face to face with his audience, Thoreau discovered the language, form, and tone necessary to transform his journal's private hymns to the gods into the art of public discourse."

Thoreau often traveled the twenty-six miles to Worcester, Massachusetts, then a town of sixteen thousand, to lecture and visit with two close friends. One was Harrison Gray Otis Blake, Harvard graduate and teacher and one of the town's leading liberals. Their close connection began in 1848, when Blake wrote Thoreau in praise of one of his essays in the *Dial*. By this means, Thoreau won his first major disciple and began the most important correspondence of his life. During the fourteen years remaining to him, Thoreau wrote some fifty letters to Blake. The letters were so extraordinary that Blake would invite friends over to his home to share them.

Thoreau and Blake's was a correspondence given to philosophical issues, not intimate exchanges. The letters bring out the principles that Thoreau is best remembered for—self-reliance, enjoyment of nature, courage, morality. In his first letter, Thoreau said, "Do what you love. Know your own bone; gnaw at it, bury

Thoreau addressed spiritual matters in an extraordinary set of fifty letters written to Harrison Gray Otis Blake, a former Unitarian minister who initiated their thirteen-year correspondence in 1848 in his only extant letter.

it, unearth it, and gnaw it still. Do not be too moral. You cheat yourself out of much life so. Aim above morality. Be not *simply* good—be good for something." So helpful are they to understanding Thoreau that these remarkable letters were recently published in one volume.

Thoreau's other Worcester friend was Theophilus Brown, a tailor known as the wit of Worcester. Blake and Brown organized many lectures for Thoreau, held in Blake's parlor or in local halls for larger audiences. Thoreau gave nine lectures in Worcester, more than in any other place but Concord, where he delivered twenty-six.

Emerson, on his own speaking tours, encouraged lyceum managers to invite his friend Thoreau. Thoreau saw in Emerson how a strong literary reputation could be built on the lecture platform. Hawthorne too helped out by inviting Thoreau to lecture at the lyceum in Salem, where he now

Known for his keen wit and original thinking, Theophilus Brown was an admirer of Henry Thoreau and the other Concord Transcendentalists. He often hosted them when they visited Worcester, Massachusetts.

lived. The *Salem Observer* reviewed Thoreau's talk, saying, "It was done in an admirable manner, in a strain of exquisite humor, with a strong undercurrent of delicate satire against the follies of the times."

What Thoreau had to say was sometimes drawn from his *Walden* manuscript in the making. But *Walden* was published so much later, that the lecture tour had little impact on its sales.

Chapter Twelve

OTHER LIVES TO LIVE

TWO YEARS, two months, and two days after going to live at Walden Pond, Thoreau left there. The reason? It seemed to be because Emerson, who planned to go abroad for a lecture tour in England, asked that Thoreau come to look after his house and family. And this, Thoreau, who remembered fondly his life with the Emersons before he went to Staten Island, was glad to do.

But he had another reason to leave the pond. For he had not only written *A Week on the Concord and Merrimack Rivers*—and a large part of a second book, *Walden*—but he had other lives to live. He tells us:

> I left the woods for as good a reason as I went there. Perhaps it seemed to me that I had several more lives to live, and could not spare any more time for that one. It is remarkable how easily and insensibly we fall into a particular route, and make a beaten track for ourselves. I had not lived there a week before my feet wore a path from my door to the pond-side; and

though it is five or six years since I trod it, it is still quite distinct. It is true, I fear, that others may have fallen into it, and so helped to keep it open. The surface of the earth is soft and impressible by the feet of men; and so with the paths which the mind travels. How worn and dusty, then, must be the highways of the world, how deep the ruts of tradition and conformity! I did not wish to take a cabin passage, but rather to go before the mast and on the deck of the world, for there I could best see the moonlight amid the mountains. I do not wish to go below now.

I learned this, at least, by my experiment: that if one advances confidently in the direction of his dreams, and endeavors to live the life which he has imagined, he will meet with a success unexpected in common hours. He will put some things behind, will pass an invisible boundary; new, universal, and more liberal laws will begin to establish themselves around and within him; or the old laws be expanded, and interpreted in his favor in a more liberal sense, and he will live with the license of a higher order of beings. In proportion as he simplifies his life, the laws of the universe will appear less complex, and solitude will not be solitude, nor poverty poverty, nor weakness weakness. If you have built castles in the air, your work need not be lost; that is where they should be. Now put the foundations under them.

Thoreau moved back into the Emerson home in October 1847. That fall he took walks with Channing and Alcott. In November he discouraged the hopes of Sophia Foord, fifteen years his senior, who wanted to marry him. She was active both as a transcendentalist and an abolitionist. The year before, she had tutored the Emerson and Alcott children, and she had fallen in love with Thoreau. Ill health forced her to give up teaching, and she returned to her home in Milton, Massachusetts. It was six

Both Emerson and his wife considered their Concord home (above) *as an intellectual center. Thus they often had long-term residents joining them, among them Henry David Thoreau, whose somewhat unusual household role ranged from handyman to close friend and confidant to Mrs. Emerson.*

months later that she proposed to him. She confided to a friend that she thought herself Thoreau's soul's twin, and that she expected to be united with him in heaven if not on this earth. She would outlive Thoreau by twenty years and never marry but remain devoted to him to the end.

Foord was not the only woman who set her heart on Thoreau. Interviews with some of his close friends disclosed that at least one other had been "quite willing, even anxious" to link her life with his.

Thoreau picked up the chores he had long carried out for the

Emersons. He did the needed repairs, put up shelves, replaced broken picket fencing, and in the spring, he manured the fields and planted the garden. His greatest pleasure came from the time devoted to the Emerson children: Ellen, now eight; Edith, six; and Edward, three. He took them boating on Walden Pond, helped them gather wildflowers, and taught them not to fear snakes and how to handle them. Eddy so delighted in his older companion that he asked if Thoreau could be his father. From England, Emerson wrote his wife about how comforting it was to know that Thoreau was watching over his family.

In England, Emerson spread word that Thoreau was a great man they would hear of by and by. When Emerson returned home in July 1848, Thoreau moved back into his family's house. To help out, he took on odd jobs, pitched in at the pencil factory, continued his surveying, and gave some lectures out of town. Horace Greeley helped promote his lyceum appearances with an editorial in his *Tribune*. He described Thoreau as "a young student, who has imbibed (or rather has refused to stifle) the idea that a man's soul is better worth living for than his body."

Meanwhile, Thoreau was trying to find someone who would publish *A Week*. While living at the Emersons, he had sent it to four publishers. All of them refused it, unless he would pay the cost of publication up front. He kept revising and expanding that book, as well as *Walden*. Finally, Thoreau tried James Munroe, a Boston publisher. Munroe agreed to do *A Week*, but only if Thoreau would pay the cost of production if the book didn't sell. They would follow *A Week* with *Walden*.

Thoreau concluded that he couldn't do better than Munroe's offer. He signed the contract and was soon correcting proofs. Just as the book was nearing publication, his elder sister, Helen Thoreau, fell desperately sick. She had been gradually wasting away with tuberculosis, and Thoreau saw that she was doomed. No one knew what to do about that dreaded, almost universal plague.

Although all four of the Thoreau children were well educated, Helen, a Concord Academy graduate, seems to have been the one best able to hold her own intellectually with her brother Henry. He once wrote her a chatty family letter—in Latin.

On May 30, 1849, *A Week* was published. Two weeks later, Greeley placed a long and favorable review on the front page of his *Tribune*. The very next day, June 14, Helen Thoreau died. She was only thirty-six. It was but seven years after Thoreau had lost his brother John. Helen was buried next to John.

A few months later, Thoreau wrote Harvard president Jared Sparks to request permission to borrow books from Harvard's library. As if to state a firm commitment, he added, "I have chosen letters as my profession." This didn't mean that writing was now his only occupation. He continued to take on surveying jobs. The family business by this time had changed from making pencils to supplying powdered graphite (a substance used in pencils) to electrotypers—a new (1840) printing technology. This transition proved profitable enough for the Thoreaus to buy a large house on Main Street, which Thoreau renovated. All this, with lectures in Concord and beyond.

Reviews of *A Week* began to trickle in. The book did not get a great send-off. His friends generally admired the book. Some periodicals showed only lukewarm enthusiasm. Yet one reviewer called it "a rare work in American literature," and another said it was "a remarkable volume and its author a remarkable man." It was hard to know how to take this odd book. For it was not just the travel story its title suggested. No, it was chock-full of many independent essays on a variety of subjects, from friendship and Chaucer to Christianity, Oriental literature, history, Sir Walter Raleigh, geological potholes, Goethe, and cattle shows. It seems

Although the original edition of A Week on the Concord and Merrimack Rivers *did not sell at the time, the book is still in print today. Modern readers view the mixture of essay, poetry, and travel writing as a predecessor to* Walden, *expressing Thoreau's developing views on humanity's place in the natural order of things.*

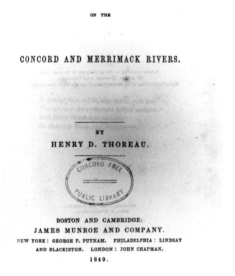

A WEEK

ON THE

CONCORD AND MERRIMACK RIVERS.

BY

HENRY D. THOREAU.

BOSTON AND CAMBRIDGE:
JAMES MUNROE AND COMPANY.
NEW YORK: GEORGE P. PUTNAM.   PHILADELPHIA: LINDSAY
AND BLACKISTON.   LONDON: JOHN CHAPMAN.
1849.

REVIEWS OF NEW BOOKS.

H. D. Thoreau's Book.

A WEEK ON THE CONCORD AND MERRIMAC RIVERS. By HENRY D. THOREAU, (pp. 413. 12mo.) Boston: Munroe & Co. New York: G. P. Putnam.

A really new book—a fresh, original, thoughtful work—is sadly rare in this age of omniferous publication. Mr. Thoreau's, if not entirely this, is very near it. Its observations of Nature are as genial as Nature herself, and the tones of his harp have an Æolian sweetness. His reflections are always striking, often profoundly truthful, and his scholastic treasures, though a little too ostentatiously displayed, are such as the best instructed reader will enjoy and thank him for. His philosophy, which is the Pantheistic egotism vaguely characterised as Transcendental, does not delight us. It seems second-hand, imitative, often exaggerated—a bad specimen of a dubious and dangerous school. But we will speak first of the staple of the work.

Mr. Thoreau is a native and resident of Concord, Mass.—a scholar, a laborer, and in some sort a hermit. He traveled somewhat in his earlier years (he is still young,) generally trusting to his own thoughts for company and his walking-cane for motive power. It would seem a main purpose of his life to demonstrate how slender an impedi-

Reviews of A Week on the Concord and Merrimac Rivers *were mixed. This reviewer characterizes the book as a "fresh, original, thoughtful work," yet it is critical of Thoreau's underlying philosophy.*

that during the years his book remained unpublished, Thoreau packed it with essays the magazines didn't want.

A Week did not sell well, and Munroe insisted that Thoreau pay the cost of publication. Where would that money come from? What savings did he have? To settle the account, he had to pay Munroe $290, about a year's wages for the average workman at that time.

The publisher shipped Thoreau the unsold copies, saying there was no room for them in his cellar. A wagon soon pulled up in Concord with a load of 706 copies out of the 1,000 that had been printed. Thoreau carried them in batches up two flights of stairs to his workroom. In his journal he notes wryly, "I have now a library of nearly 900 volumes, over 700 of which I wrote myself. Is it not well that the author should behold the fruits of his labor?" Some copies he managed to sell himself, and he gave away about 75.

Over the rest of his life Thoreau would sell a copy here and a copy there, at $1.25, until 1862, when Boston publisher Ticknor and Fields purchased the remaining copies. Shortly after Thoreau's death later that year, Ticknor and Fields reissued those copies with a new title page, calling it a second edition. The book has been in print ever since, but it has never achieved the success of *Walden*.

Chapter Thirteen

Pioneer in Conservation

DUE TO *A Week*'s failure to sell, Thoreau was unable to have *Walden* published for another five years. During that long interval, he rewrote many passages and added others. Perhaps to comfort himself, he says in *Walden*, "The life which men praise and regard as successful is but one kind. Why should we exaggerate any one kind at the expense of the others?"

His disappointment with *A Week* led Thoreau to concentrate on his nature writing and his travel pieces rather than philosophical essays. Facing an audience at his lectures, he learned to find the language and tone that would reach their minds and hearts.

Thoreau's travels gave him his most popular material. While still at Walden Pond, he had made the first of several trips to the Maine woods. He was swept along by the romantic interest in the wilderness that sparked the American imagination in that era. The vast yet-to-be-explored regions of the continent, empty (they thought) of people and of civilization seemed divine. Yet would all this be destroyed by the rapid growth of commercial and industrial power?

Greeley placed Thoreau's essay, "Ktaadn and the Maine Woods," on that trip to Maine in the new *Union* magazine, which ran it in five installments. It surprised readers, for it set a frontier story not in the Wild West but in the East. Thoreau described what he saw and did it in fresh, realistic detail.

Thoreau made several trips to Cape Cod, that long arm of Massachusetts embracing the Atlantic shore. He wrote essays on those trips that were published in book form after his death. Called *Cape Cod*, this book is his sunniest, most lighthearted work. On his return from the first visit, he lectured on it at the

KTAADN, AND THE MAINE WOODS.

BY HENRY D. THOREAU.

No. I.

THE WILDS OF THE PENOBSCOT.

On the 31st of August, 1846, I left Concord in Massachusetts for Bangor and the backwoods of Maine, by way of the railroad and steamboat, intending to accompany a relative of mine engaged in the lumber trade in Bangor, as far as a dam on the west branch of the Penobscot, in which property he was interested. From this place, which is about one hundred miles by the river above Bangor, thirty miles from the Houlton military road, and five miles beyond the last log hut, I proposed to make excursions to mount Ktaadn, the second highest mountain in New England, about thirty miles distant, and some of the lakes of the Penobscot, either alone or with such company as I might pick up there. It is unusual to find a camp so far in the woods at that season, when lumbering operations have ceased, and I was glad to avail myself of the circumstance of a

mountainous region of the State of Maine stretches from near the White Mountains, northeasterly one hundred and sixty miles, to the head of the Aroostook river, and is about sixty miles wide. The wild or unsettled portion is far more extensive. So that some hours only of travel in this direction will carry the curious to the verge of a primitive forest, more interesting, perhaps, on all accounts, than they would reach by going a thousand miles westward.

The next forenoon, Tuesday, Sept. 1st, I started with my companion in a buggy from Bangor for " up river," expecting to be overtaken the next day night, at Mattawamkeag Point, some sixty miles off, by two more Bangoreans, who had decided to join us in a trip to the mountain. We had each a knapsack or bag filled with such clothing and articles as were indispensable, and my compan-

On his trips to Maine, the ever-curious, highly observant Thoreau was able to identify several plants and even some trees that he had not observed in Massachusetts.

Concord Lyceum. The lecture was a great success. A delightful section dealt with John Newcomb, an old Wellfleet, Massachusetts, oysterman who could entertain people for hours with stories of the Cape and the sea.

But there was grim reality too. On the first trip, Thoreau and Ellery Channing learned that just before their arrival, a violent storm had wrecked a ship offshore, costing the lives of 145 Irish immigrants. Thoreau did not spare his audience what he saw on the Cape beach as high waves continued to wash ashore the victims of the shipwreck. He saw

> many marble feet and matted heads as the cloths were raised, and one livid, swollen and mangled body of a drowned girl,—who probably had intended to go out to service in some American family,—to which some rags still adhered, with a string, half concealed by the flesh, about its swollen neck; the coiled up wreck of a human hulk, gashed by the rocks or fishes, so that the bone and muscle were exposed, but quite bloodless,—merely red and white, with wide open and staring eyes, yet lustreless, dead-lights; or like the cabin windows of a stranded vessel, filled with sand.

In 1851 Thoreau turned thirty-four. Noting the birthday in his journal, he wrote, "I think that no experience which I have today comes up to, or is comparable with, the experiences of my youth. I can remember that I was all alive, and inhabited my body with inexpressible satisfaction."

This was more than 150 years ago, when most people died much younger than people do now. Then, too, Thoreau had recently gone to the dentist, who found it necessary to remove all Thoreau's teeth under ether and replace them with a set of false teeth. "Art outdoes Nature!" Thoreau told Emerson, pleased with the result.

Not long before, a coolness had tempered the relationship between Emerson and Thoreau. They remained friends, but their intimacy faded. The older man was nearing the end of his most creative period, whereas Thoreau was still climbing upward. Perhaps Thoreau felt he needed to become more independent, to stand on his own. They saw less of each other, though Emerson still sent odd jobs Thoreau's way.

You can't think of Thoreau as getting old when you know that afternoons, he took walks of fifteen to twenty miles, gone sometimes for four hours. When he planned on long expeditions, he carried a knapsack of India-rubber cloth he'd made himself, partitioned to fit in books, papers, a spyglass, a measuring tape, and sewing equipment.

Further equipped, hooked over his arm was a huge umbrella. He built a special shelf into the hat he wore to carry botanical specimens he gathered on the way. He was always on the watch for birds, bees, wasps, frogs, toads, and flowers, keeping a pocket diary of plants due to bloom.

*Thoreau collected these specimens of lillies (*Lilium canadense*) in 1857. In the 1850s, Thoreau collected approximately nine hundred plant specimens from the New England area. His collection is housed at Harvard's Gray Herbarium.*

The Indians

Native Americans were still a familiar sight around Concord when Thoreau was a child. In the fall of 1850, people in the Penobscot nation camped along the Concord River when they came to sell baskets, and Thoreau went over to visit. Whether near home or out on his expeditions, he would find Indian artifacts, especially stone arrowheads, spear points, and axes.

In 1850 Thoreau began his first "Indian Book." It was not for publication, but as a place to store the facts and quotations culled from the more than two hundred books he had read on Indian life. Over the years, he would fill eleven manuscript notebooks, totaling twenty-eight hundred pages and half a million words.

Thoreau planned his expeditions to the Maine woods in the hope of getting to know more about Indian life and history in their native habitat. He always hired an Indian guide, asking the guide to tell him all the guide knew. One of these guides was Joe Aitten, a native leader. One night Thoreau camped with a group of Indians, watching them cure their moose hides and smoke the meat. They talked for hours after they all bedded down, with Thoreau asking them to tell him the meaning of the Indian words.

For another Maine canoe trip, Thoreau hired Joseph Polis, a Penobscot leader, who met Thoreau in Bangor carrying an eighteen-foot canoe on his head. Thoreau had the guide teach him as much of his language as he could, and the Indian name for everything they saw, from herbs to streams and from mountains to paddles. Before they fell asleep in their tents, Polis entertained Thoreau with musical Indian chants. That canoe journey covered 325 miles.

Thoreau believed that scientists could enlarge their knowledge and understanding if they paid more attention to the Indians and their languages and habits. But he was not alone in his serious study of the Indian. At least three other scholars published books on their findings on Indian history in that decade. What Thoreau learned he described in "The Allegash and East Branch," published after his death as a section in *The Maine Woods*. "Allegash" has been called one of the best portraits of the Native American by a white writer in nineteenth-century American literature. In it Thoreau gives us the experience of wilderness. It was still another way he advanced the cause of conservation.

Although it was Thoreau's intent to totally immerse himself in Maine's natural history, he found himself equally fascinated with the historic Penobscot people. This photo shows a Penobscot tribal leader wearing ceremonial attire.

When his old rowboat wore out with heavy usage in 1852, Thoreau got a new one. He considered the water he rowed over his private farm. In a journal entry of April 16, 1852, he reported his experience in cornering a woodchuck away from its hole:

> I squatted down and surveyed him at my leisure. . . . When I moved, it gritted its teeth quite loud, sometimes striking the under jaw against the other chatteringly, sometimes grinding one jaw on the other, yet as if more from instinct than anger. Whichever way I turned, that way it headed. I took a twig a good long one and touched its snout, at which it started forward and bit the stick, lessening the distance between us by two feet, and still it held all the ground it gained. I played with it tenderly awhile with the stick, trying to open its gritting jaws. . . . We sat looking at one another about half an hour, till he began to feel mesmeric influences. . . . I walked round him; he turned as fast and fronted me still. I sat down by his side within a foot. I talked to him quasi forest lingo, baby-talk, at any rate in a conciliatory tone, and thought that I had some influence on him. He gritted his teeth less. . . . With a little stick I lifted one of his paws to examine it, and held it up at pleasure. I turned him over to see what color he was beneath (darker or more purely brown), though he turned himself back again sooner than I could have wished. . . . I spoke kindly to him. I reached checkerberry leaves to his mouth. I stretched my hands over him, though he turned up his head and still gritted a little. I laid my hand on him, but immediately took it off again, instinct not being wholly overcome. If I had had a few fresh bean leaves, thus in advance of the season, I am sure I should have tamed him completely. . . . I finally had to leave him without seeing him move from the place.

America was becoming more science-minded in that era. By this time, the older word *naturalist* was displaced by the new word *scientist*. Thoreau became so meticulous in recording what he observed that in a period of ten years, he located more than eight hundred of the known botanical species of his county.

Thoreau's greatest contribution to scientific knowledge is the essay "The Succession of Forest Trees." For years he had tried to figure out why and how trees and plants spring up. His careful notes on his observations on the dispersal of seeds by animal, bird, wind, and human piled up. Finally he concluded that though the great variety of seeds spread in all directions, only a few take root, and even fewer meet the conditions needed for them to mature. His findings, published widely, proved valid and useful to good forest management.

His shelves were stacked with technical field books and handbooks on every kind of plant and animal life. Yet he seemed to fear science might drain the blood out of life, destroy the beauty, the poetry.

The Concord folk came to realize what an authority lived in their midst. If someone found something extraordinary in nature, they'd come to Thoreau for an explanation. He was glad to answer when he could and ready to do the research for them if he didn't have the answer.

In the 1850s, Thoreau saw the birth of the modern biological sciences as well as Charles Darwin's theory of evolution. Harvard created the Lawrence Scientific School, with Louis Agassiz the professor of zoology and geology. Thoreau collected new species for the professor, who acknowledged those contributions.

In the early 1850s Thoreau prepared two new lectures, "Walking" and "The Wild," published years later in the *Atlantic Monthly*. The lectures were his plea to preserve at least some wilderness for the generations to come. Modern advocates of conservation value them as seminal documents. His declaration in those lectures—"In wildness is the preservation of the world"—might be their motto.

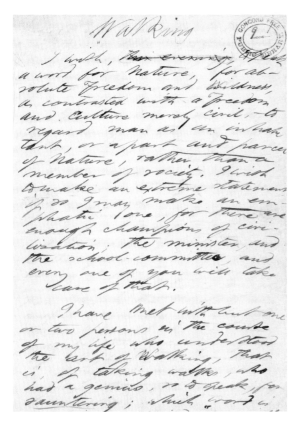

"Walking," which began as a lecture delivered by Thoreau at the Concord Lyceum in 1851, contains the quotation, "In wildness is the preservation of the world," a phrase that has become one of the rallying cries of the environmental movement. The lecture was eventually developed into an essay and was published in the Atlantic Monthly *a month after Thoreau's death.*

The many excursions Thoreau made never interrupted for too long his study of the natural history of his hometown. Concord's children loved to help by gathering specimens for him. Birds' eggs especially, but also birds' nests. Once, even a live little heron. Adults too were eager to bring him their discoveries, and he recorded their gifts: hawk, loon, sandpiper, snipe.

Chapter Fourteen

RESCUING FUGITIVE SLAVES

FOR THE GREAT MAJORITY of Northerners, slavery was some remote condition in Southern states or in the West Indies. Nothing to be bothered about. Only crackpots or fanatics let it keep them up nights. That was not Thoreau. He knew how slavery's tentacles reached out to poison life in the North too. Right here in his own state, thousands of Massachusetts women and children made palm-leaf hats to be shipped South for use by slaves. And thousands more workers labored in New England's textile mills, manufacturing cotton goods made cheap by the unpaid labor of blacks on Southern cotton plantations. Thoreau had gone to jail for refusing to pay his taxes and had written "Civil Disobedience" in protest against the Mexican War, waged on behalf of slaveholders who wished to extend slave territory.

As the 1850s began, the political pot came to a boil. Should the immense western territories carved out of Mexico come into the Union as slave states or free states? Should the slave trade be allowed to continue? Could slave owners reclaim runaways who fled to freedom in the North?

In Congress a great debate took place to settle the urgent questions. By the fall of 1850, a compromise (in favor of the South) was reached. The territories carved out of Mexico would decide the slavery question for themselves. California would enter the Union as a free state. The foreign slave trade would be killed, but not slavery in the District of Columbia, where the nation's capital sat. A new and harsher fugitive slave law would force the North to return fugitive slaves.

Thoreau saw slavery as the central issue of his time. For many years, he had spoken and acted against it. So had his family and several neighbors. His sister Helen and his Aunt Maria were members of the Women's Anti-Slavery Society. Concord was long a center for Underground Railroad activity. Several people were "stationmasters" who sheltered fugitive slaves and helped them on their flight to freedom. In *Walden*, Thoreau describes runaway slaves brought to his cabin "who listened from time to time . . . as if they heard hounds baying on their track, and looked at me beseechingly, as much as to say,—'O Christian, will you send me back?'"

Since the tiny cabin in which he lived during this period had no room for concealment, Thoreau would smuggle the fugitives into town to his mother's house during the night. From there he would help them on their way to Canada, often giving them money from his scarce funds.

The new Fugitive Slave Law adopted by Congress made the penalties for helping slaves to escape very heavy. A thousand-dollar fine was imposed, an immense sum in that time. And the law ordered everyone to help the slave-catchers. Only a few months after passage of that law, a Concord blacksmith named Francis Bigelow defied the law to help send Shadrach, an escaped Virginia slave who was working as a Boston waiter, to Canada and

Thomas Sims escaped slavery in Georgia and was later arrested in Boston under the federal Fugitive Slave Law. The legal decision to return him to his owner became a cause célèbre (famous case) for the Massachusetts abolitionist movement. A huge contingent of police (shown here) *escorted Sims from Boston.*

freedom. In April, rescuers tried desperately, but failed, to prevent the return of a Georgia slave, seventeen-year-old Thomas Sims. Thoreau exploded in anger at the government. So did his fellow writers—Emerson, Lowell, and Whittier.

Hardly six months later, Thoreau himself defied the Fugitive Slave Law. At 5:00 P.M. on October 1, 1851, he recorded the incident in his journal:

> Just put a fugitive slave, who has taken the name of Henry Williams, into the cars for Canada. He escaped from Stafford County, Virginia, to Boston last October; has been in Shadrach's place at the Cornhill Coffee-House; had been corresponding

through an agent with his master, who is his father, about buying himself, his master asking $600, but he having been able to raise only $500. Heard that there were writs out for two Williamses, fugitives, and was informed by his fellow-servants and employer that Augerhole Burns and others of the police had called for him when he was out. Accordingly fled to Concord last night on foot, bringing a letter to our family from Mr. Lovejoy of Cambridge and another which Garrison had formerly given him on another occasion. He lodged with us, and waited in the house till funds were collected with which to forward him. Intended to dispatch him at noon through to Burlington, but when I went to buy his ticket, saw one at the depot who looked and behaved so much like a Boston policeman that I did not venture that time. An intelligent and very well-behaved man, a mulatto.

The slave said he could guide himself by many other stars than the north star, whose rising and setting he knew. They steered for the north star even when it got round and appeared to them to be in the south. They frequently followed the telegraph when there was no railroad. The slaves bring many superstitions from Africa. The fugitives sometimes superstitiously carry a turf in their hats, thinking that their success depends on it.

It was another such occasion, in midsummer 1853, that Moncure Conway, the liberal young son of a Southern slave-owner, observed on a visit to the Thoreau house:

When I went to the house next morning, I found them all [Thoreau was then living in his father's house] in a state of excitement by reason of the arrival of a fugitive Negro from the South, who had come fainting to their door about daybreak and thrown himself on their mercy. Thoreau took me in to see the poor wretch, whom I found to be a man with whose face as that of a slave in the South I was familiar. The Negro was much terrified at seeing me, supposing that I was one of his pursuers. Having quieted his fears by the assurance that I too, though in a different sense, was a refugee from the bondage he was escaping, and at the same time being able to attest the Negro's genuineness, I sat and watched the singularly tender and lowly devotion of the scholar to the slave. He must be fed, his swollen feet bathed; and he must think of nothing but rest. Again and again this coolest and calmest of men drew near to the trembling Negro, and bade him feel at home, and have no fear that any power should again wrong him. He could not walk that day, but must mount guard over the fugitive, for slavehunters were not extinct in those days; and so I went away after a while much impressed by many little traits that I had seen as they had appeared in this emergency. . . .

Hardly a week went by in that time without people of Concord sheltering some fugitive overnight and helping him or her on his or her way before daylight. Henry Thoreau, they agreed, did more than any other man in Concord to help.

Nothing angered Thoreau more than the rescue case that began on the night of May 24, 1854, when a fugitive slave, Anthony Burns, was arrested by a marshal in Boston. Within twenty-four hours, the city was in an uproar. The Reverend Thomas Wentworth Higginson led a small band who tried to batter down the doors of the courthouse to free the fugitive jailed inside. Police officers held them off until troops and artillery were called out to keep order. The rescue mission failed, and Burns was sent back to his master in Virginia.

That event won an army of converts to the antislavery cause. As public anger mounted, the abolitionists held their annual Fourth of July celebration in Framingham, Massachusetts.

The Reverend Thomas Wentworth Higgins was not only an avid abolitionist but also a strong advocate for equal opportunity and rights for women. He is shown here with his young daughter in about 1884.

Garrison, to show his contempt for "the proslavery laws and deeds of the nation," held aloft a copy of the Constitution and, calling it "a covenant with death and an agreement with Hell," burned it to ashes.

Thoreau was one of the speakers at that meeting. His powerful speech, "Slavery in Massachusetts," attacked both press and church as defenders of slavery, and appealed to the nation for a higher standard of morality. He traced the connections among politics, business, and the dehumanizing effect of slavery:

Thoreau's home state of Massachusetts was a strong center of abolitionism. The state was the first to abolish slavery outright back in 1781. The etching above shows an antislavery rally in Worcester.

If I were seriously to propose to Congress to make mankind into sausages, I have no doubt that most of the members would smile at my proposition. . . . But if any of them will tell me that to make a man into a sausage would be much worse,—would be any worse, than to make him into a slave—than it was to enact the Fugitive Slave Law, I will accuse him of foolishness, of intellectual incapacity, of making a distinction without a difference.

He was forcing people to realize that both sausages and slaves are treated by their government simply as commodities, traded and then consumed by the plantation economy. Northerners who supported the Fugitive Slave Law were taking part in that marketplace, which Thoreau saw as an act of cannibalism.

In his "Civil Disobedience" essay, Thoreau had criticized lawyers and politicians for bowing down to "consistency" or precedent rather than truth. Now, he told his audience, is "no time to be judging according to . . . precedents, but to establish a precedent for the future."

He was putting the issue before the country in the starkest terms. He was ready to accept and to practice violence. "I need not say what match I would touch, what system endeavor to blow up—but as I love my life, I would side with the light, and let the dark earth roll from under me, calling my mother and my brother to follow."

"My thoughts are murder to the State," wrote Thoreau. "The law will never make men free; it is men who have got to make the law free. They are the lovers of law and order who observe the law when the government breaks it." He was publicly denouncing both Church and State for accepting slavery and even supporting it.

The time to argue over abstract principles was gone. Now was the time to act.

The revolt against the Fugitive Slave Law was a turning point for many in Massachusetts who had long been indifferent or even hostile to the antislavery movement. The state legislature passed a Personal Liberty Law, which made it almost impossible to send fugitive slaves back into bondage.

Chapter Fifteen

"LIFE WITHOUT PRINCIPLE"

THERE ARE SENTENCES, paragraphs, in Thoreau's journal that seem to suggest that he suffered from periods of depression. They stand out in contrast to his joy in nature and its capacity for renewal. It would seem he lost faith in people.

You could not say that this was typical of him. Political institutions rigged against human needs, government's failure to do what he considered right and moral, surely disappointed Thoreau. Then, too, there was the cooling of his friendship with Emerson and perhaps with other friends.

It was clear that his book, *A Week*, was going nowhere in sales. And thus far, attempts to get *Walden* published had failed. But there was another element: modern medicine has found that tuberculosis—which harassed Thoreau from childhood—may cause or intensify depression. Again and again the disease flared up: in 1836, in 1841, in 1843. And in the spring of 1855, a puzzling weakness of the legs—probably linked to tuberculosis—would make him give up his daily walk for several months.

Meeting Walt Whitman

A surveying job in New Jersey led Thoreau to a memorable meeting in 1856 with the poet Walt Whitman. Each writer had, within a twelve-month period, published an American classic—Thoreau, *Walden*, and Whitman, *Leaves of Grass*. Bronson Alcott, then staying in New York, brought Thoreau to the Whitman home in Brooklyn. They began talking in Whitman's bedroom upstairs and then moved to the living room below. At first both were shy and reserved. But they soon warmed, with Thoreau asking questions about *Leaves of Grass*. "Whitman," he said, "do you have any idea that you are bigger and outside the average—may perhaps have immense significance?"

Alcott observed that Whitman and Thoreau acted warily, "like two beasts, each wondering what the other would do, whether to

Walt Whitman is known as one of America's greatest poets, but, like Thoreau, he was not considered a success by the standards of the society in which he lived.

snap or run." Whitman said he lived to make his poems and "for nothing else particularly." He spent his mornings reading and writing and his afternoons walking—a program much like Thoreau's. Whitman gave Thoreau a copy of the new edition of *Leaves*. Later Thoreau wrote his Worcester friend, Blake, that he thought *Leaves* was "an incomparable sermon . . . a great primitive poem, an alarm or trumpet-note ringing through the American camp. . . . By his heartiness and broad generalities he puts me into a liberal frame of mind prepared to see wonders. . . . He is apparently the greatest democrat the world has seen."

About the sensual passages in *Leaves* (an excerpt is below), Thoreau said Whitman "has spoken more truth than any American or modern that I know. I have found his poem exhilarating, encouraging. . . . We ought to rejoice greatly in him."

Are you the new person drawn toward me? To begin with take warning, I am surely far different from what you suppose; Do you suppose you will find in me your ideal? Do you think it so easy to have me become your lover? Do you think the friendship of me would be unalloy'd satisfaction? Do you think I am trusty and faithful? Do you see no further than this facade, this smooth and tolerant manner of me? Do you suppose yourself advancing on real ground toward a real heroic man? Have you no thought O dreamer that it may be all my illusion?

The wonder is that throughout these bouts of illness he remained so calm and composed. His sister Sophia said, "During his long illness I never heard a murmur escape him . . . his perfect contentment was truly wonderful."

In March 1854, Thoreau finished work on an essay he called "Getting a Living," a problem or challenge everyone wrestles with. He gave it as a lecture in Providence, Rhode Island, and then in several other towns over the next few years. It reached print in the *Atlantic Monthly*, but not until after his death. And then its title was the one used now: "Life Without Principle."

In it Thoreau gets to the core of his philosophy on how to live. He asks us to get down to basics, not to be led astray by popular opinion or the desire for money or power. Follow your own inner light, he says. "The ways by which you may get money almost without exception lead downwards." You can be very busy, he points out, yet not be spending your time well. And then, "You must get your living by loving."

All the while, Thoreau worked constantly on his *Walden* manuscript. He kept making changes, cutting, adding, rewriting. By now he was on his seventh draft. Finally, in 1854, perhaps at Emerson's prodding, the young firm of Ticknor and Fields agreed to publish *Walden*. Proofs came in quickly and Thoreau made changes up to the last minute. His handwriting had become so poor that the typesetter had great trouble with it. Horace Greeley, delighted to help by building public interest in advance, published long passages from *Walden* in his *New York Daily Tribune* in July.

All this was going on while Thoreau was preparing his "Slavery in Massachusetts" speech for the 1854 Fourth of July celebration.

In August, Thoreau's journal noted:

Wednesday—To Boston
Walden published. Elder-berries. Waxwork yellowing

Walden (1854) was one of only two books by Thoreau that were published during his lifetime, the other being A Week on the Concord and Merrimack Rivers*(1849).* Walden *records Thoreau's thoughts during the time he spent living in a self-built cabin on the shore of Walden Pond.*

With *Walden* available at last, Emerson urged it on friends, writing to one, "It is cheerful, sparkling, readable, with all kinds of merits, & rising sometimes to very great heights. We accord Henry the undoubted King of all American lions. He is walking up and down Concord, firm-looking, but in a tremble of great expectation."

Hawthorne, now the American consul at Liverpool, plugged the book to his British friends. And George Eliot, the British novelist, recommended it highly in a review. About seventy reviews of *Walden* appeared, with three-fourths of them strongly favorable. Sales were modest at first, though much better than for *A Week*. Recognition of *Walden* as a masterpiece, one of the great American classics of nonfiction, came after Thoreau's death.

Walden has never gone out of print. It has appeared in more than 150 different editions, often selling in the hundreds of thousands of copies. Millions of people have bought *Walden*, and more continue to buy it. And it has continued to appear in many foreign languages: Danish, Dutch, Finnish, German, Greek, Hebrew, Italian, Japanese, Norse, Portuguese, Russian, Sanskrit, Spanish, Swedish.

Walter Harding holds that

> *Walden* can be read on many levels. . . . It is one of the outstanding nature books of all time. . . . It is a vivid exposition of the simple life that all of us at times yearn for. . . . It is a biting satire on the many, many flaws and foibles of the merry chase of life most of us are leading today. . . . But above all *Walden* is a positive book . . . a guide to the higher life . . . a plea that would we but obey that light within us we could attain a fulfillment, a happiness, and a success such as man has never known. And Thoreau in his buoyant optimism believed that man would some day achieve that goal.

Contemporary Reviews of Walden

Although many reviewers were struck by the author's eccentricity, most appreciated Thoreau's originality and eye for nature.

A very curious book is in press, entitled 'Life in the Woods,' by H. D. Thoreau. . . . The writer . . . seems to have proposed to himself to reduce his mode of life to the standard nearest to primitive nature. —*Oneida Circular* (August 1, 1854)

This is a sort of autobiography of a hermit, who lived two years alone in the woods on Concord, Mass., a mile from any neighbor. Mr. Thoreau's object . . . appears to have been . . . to ascertain by experiment, what are the absolute necessities of man. . . . It is a curious and amusing book, . . . but containing many shrewd and sensible suggestions, with a fair share of nonsense. —*Daily Evening Traveller* [Boston] (August 9, 1854)

An original book, this, and from an original man—from a very eccentric man. It is a record of the author's life and thoughts while he lived in the woods—two years and two months. . . . There is much to be learned from this volume. Stearn [sic] and good lessons in economy; contentment with a simple but noble life, and all that, and much more. . . . Get the book. You will like it. It is original and refreshing; and from the brain of a live man. —*Boston Daily Bee* (August 9, 1854)

Chapter Sixteen

Meeting John Brown

IN THE SPRING OF 1854, Congress made a move
that accelerated the downward path to civil war. It adopted the
Kansas-Nebraska Act, which abolitionist Frederick Douglass
called an open invitation to a "fierce and bitter strife." Under the
principle of "popular sovereignty," the law permitted the new territories in the West to come into the Union with or without slavery. The outcome depended on which side won a majority.

The race to settle Kansas began, with Southerners taking their
slaves along, and Northerners sending thousands of rifles in mil-
itant opposition to slavery. Angry people opposed to the new law
met in Wisconsin to organize a new political party—the
Republican Party—bound to oppose the extension of slavery.

Bloody battles between the two conflicting forces erupted in
Kansas. A proslavery mob of several hundred men raided the
town of Lawrence, burned the Free State Hotel, wrecked the newspaper office, and ransacked many homes. In retaliation, John
Brown, with his abolitionist sons and followers, attacked a group

of slaveholding settlers and shot five of them to death as a lesson of "an eye for an eye and a tooth for a tooth."

Two days before this incident, on May 22, 1856, Senator Charles Sumner of Massachusetts had been beaten unconscious with a cane by a member of the House of Representatives after making a speech in the Senate attacking the proslavery elements in Kansas. He was injured so badly it kept him out of public life for three years.

Violence, from Kansas to Washington, D.C., warned how close to civil war were the two opposing forces—those who believed in slavery and those who did not. The previous spring, 1855, young

Political turmoil in the United States was growing over the issue of slavery. The U.S. senator from Massachusetts, Charles Sumner, was a strong advocate for abolition. After an inflammatory speech he made in 1856 against Kansas's proslavery groups, he was beaten unconscious by South Carolina congressman Preston Brooks.

Frank Sanborn came to Concord to open a private school, and he boarded with the Thoreaus. He saw Thoreau almost daily for three years and later would be the first to write Thoreau's biography. In his diary, Sanborn jotted down his impression of Thoreau:

> [Thoreau] is a little under size—with a huge Emersonian nose, bluish gray eyes, brown hair, and a ruddy weather-beaten face, which reminds one of that of some shrewd and honest animal—some retired, philosophic woodchuck or magnanimous fox—He dresses very plainly—wears his collar turned over like Mr. Emerson, and often an old dress coat, broad in the skirts and by no means a fit—He walks about with a brisk rustic air, and never seems tired.

Happily, as winter came on, the weakness in Thoreau's legs faded, and he was able to go skating again. He loved to skim the ice at great speed, once clocking himself at fourteen miles per hour. He could keep going on the river for some thirty miles. Were his months of feeling like "a worthless invalid" finally over?

Sanborn was one of John Brown's ardent supporters. When Brown came east in 1857 to raise funds for his guerrilla fighters, Sanborn brought him to Concord for a brief visit with friends who might support his cause.

The Thoreaus had Sanborn and Brown come to lunch, and when Sanborn left to take care of his school, Brown and Thoreau had a long talk. Thoreau learned about the life of this Connecticut farmer, surveyor, and wool grower, sensing that here was a man willing to sacrifice his life for what he believed in.

In the evening, Brown spoke to a hundred people at the town hall about the battle for Kansas. He closed with a plea for funds. Sanborn, Emerson, and the Thoreaus all contributed, for, as Thoreau said, Brown impressed them as "a person of surpassing sense, courage, and religious earnestness. He did not conceal his hatred of slavery, and less his readiness to strike a blow for freedom at the fitting moment. I thought him equal to anything he should dare. . . . Not far from sixty, I thought him the manliest of men. . . ."

Over the next few years, Thoreau continued his excursions— to Maine, to the White Mountains, to Cape Cod. And a brief business trip for the last time to New York, to arrange a contract for the family graphite business.

But it was the natural history of Concord itself that inspired Thoreau's most intense activity: the fish, the frogs, the ducks, the snakes, the birds, the trees. He would spend so many hours in one spot, observing life in a swamp, that Emerson is said to have told Thoreau that if God had intended him to live in a swamp, he would have made him a frog.

Thoreau's father had been troubled by illness for some time. Gradually, Thoreau had taken on the burdens of the family's graphite business. He kept an eye on work at the mill and helped out with the packing of shipments. A bad cough weakened Mr. Thoreau so much he almost never left his chair or his bed. Early in 1859 he was confined to his bedroom. Henry Thoreau became his nurse, giving him the tenderest care. Finally, Thoreau's father died on February 3, 1859, at the age of seventy-one, probably of tuberculosis.

Thoreau became head of the family and manager of the graphite business. With his insatiable curiosity, he again examined the manufacturing method and figured out a way to improve the grinding mill process. In the spring, he and Emerson decided to improve a barren area beside Walden Pond, and Thoreau set out four hundred pines on two acres. The white pines would eventually develop into a beautiful grove.

Not long after planting the pine grove, Thoreau was hired to make a study of the Concord River and its dams and bridges. It kept him busy all the summer of 1859, surveying and measuring and making charts.

Despite all this activity, in 1859 he delivered more lectures than in any other year. After a lecture in Worcester, one of his young listeners, E. Harlow Russell, noted the impression Thoreau had made on him:

> [Thoreau] seemed rather less than the medium height, well-proportioned, and noticeably straight and erect. . . . His head was not large, nor did it strike me as handsome. It was covered with a full growth of rather dark hair somewhat carelessly brushed after no particular style. His face was very striking whether seen in the front or profile view. Large perceptive eyes—blue, I think, large and prominent nose; his mouth, concealed by a full dark beard, worn natural but not untrimmed; these features pervaded by a wise, serious and dignified look. The expression of his countenance was not severe or commanding, but it certainly gave no hint of shallowness or trifling. In speech he was deliberate and positive. The emphatic words seemed to "hang fire" or to be held back for an instant as if to gather force and weight. . . . Thoreau was always interesting, often entertaining, but never what you would call charming.

Chapter Seventeen

Raid on Harpers Ferry

ON THE RAINY SUNDAY NIGHT of October 16, 1859, John Brown, with a group of twenty-one men, five of them African Americans, attacked the federal arsenal at Harpers Ferry in Virginia. His aim was to capture the arsenal, distribute arms to the slaves in the vicinity, and spread the revolt from there across the South. The arsenal was taken, but the plan failed. President Buchanan called out marines and cavalry. Brown and several others were wounded, two of Brown's sons and eight others were killed, and the others escaped.

When the news of the raid was flashed to the country, it was as much a surprise to Thoreau as to all. Of course, proslavery people were enraged, and some abolitionists called it a misguided or even an insane effort.

But Thoreau felt the truth about John Brown, the meaning of his act, had to be made clear. On October 30 he sent a messenger to tell the people of Concord he would speak about John Brown that night in the town hall.

On October 16, 1859, abolitionist John Brown and a number of followers seized the United States Armory and Arsenal at Harpers Ferry. This raid and the ensuing capture and execution of Brown brought attention to the sharp disagreement among the United States citizenry in regard to the morality and legality of slavery.

Thoreau wanted his "Plea for Captain John Brown"—one of the first public defenses—to reach as far as possible. He gave the ninety-minute speech again in Boston, and then in Worcester, trying meanwhile to get people to write Governor Wise of Virginia, urging clemency for Brown. A half-dozen newspapers carried portions of his speech.

Asked by an official, "Upon what principle do you justify your acts?" Brown replied:

Upon the golden rule, I pity the poor in bondage that have none to help them; that is why I am here; not to gratify any personal animosity, revenge, or vindictive spirit. It is my sympathy with the oppressed and wronged, that are as good as you and precious in the sight of God.

Tried for treason, Brown and the other survivors of the raid were condemned to death. On December 2, the day of execution, Brown scrawled on a sheet of paper he left with his jailer, "I, John Brown, am now quite certain that the crimes of this guilty land will never be purged away but with blood. I had, as I now think vainly, flattered myself that without very much bloodshed it might be done." As he was taken to the scaffold on that sunny morning, Brown looked at the Blue Ridge Mountains in the distance and commented on the beauty of the country.

John Brown (center, kissing child) *was executed in Charles Town, Virginia, on December 2, 1858. As he was walking to the scaffold, he made an accurate prediction about the effect the national division over slavery would eventually have on the nation: "I, John Brown, am now quite certain that the crimes of this guilty land will never be purged away but with blood."*

On John Brown

Henry David Thoreau: "These men, in teaching us how to die, have at the same time taught us how to live."

Wendell Phillips: "He sleeps in the blessings of the crushed and the poor, and men believe more firmly in virtue, now that such a man has lived."

Louisa May Alcott: "The execution of Saint John the Just took place today."

Ralph Waldo Emerson: "I wish we might have health enough to know virtue when we see it, and not cry with the fools 'madman' when a hero passes."

John Brown

Frederick Douglass: "To his own soul he was right, and neither principalities nor powers, life nor death, things present nor things to come could shake his dauntless spirit or move him from his ground."

William Lloyd Garrison: "In firing his gun, John Brown has merely told us what time of day it is. It is high noon, thank God!"

After the capture and hanging of John Brown for his raid on Harpers Ferry, Virginia, officials from the state traveled to Massachusetts to find Frank Sanborn and return him to Virginia in order to question him about being an accomplice of Brown. As the deputies tried to grab Sanborn (above), virtually the entire town of Concord came to his aid.

To Thoreau, John Brown was a hero who followed his own conscience. He had seen that the government, in the hands of the slaveholders, had placed its power on the side of injustice. Such a government should not be obeyed. "The only government that I recognize,—and it matters not how few are at the head of it, or how small its army,—is that power which establishes justice in the land, never that which establishes injustice."

Slavery was wrong. Every peaceful way of abolishing it that had been tried had failed. If force was now required, then a man of principle, a John Brown, must not hesitate to use it. Thoreau had come to that stage of thinking gradually. "It was his [John

Brown's] peculiar doctrine that a man had a perfect right to interfere by force with the slaveholder, in order to rescue the slave. I agree with him." And soon, very soon, only the force of the Union Army would end slavery in the United States.

Brown's body was brought north by train, to be buried in North Elba, New York, where his family lived. Unable to make the trip for the memorial service, Thoreau prepared an address—"The Last Days of John Brown"—to be read there by a friend. It was a passionate defense of Brown's life as a principled struggle against the evil of slavery.

After Brown's death, his widow enrolled their daughters in Sanborn's school in Concord. They told Bronson Alcott that Thoreau reminded them of their father.

Chapter Eighteen

NOW COMES GOOD SAILING

AFTER THE DEATH of John Brown, Thoreau returned to his study of natural history. Early in 1860, he acquired a copy of the epochal new book by the British scientist Charles Darwin. He read *The Origin of Species* carefully, making extracts from it. He knew Darwin's earlier work, *Voyage of the Beagle*, and by now was thinking along the line of natural selection, a major aspect of the theory of evolution.

He gave two lectures that winter on wild apples. With the coming of spring, he began to put his journal and extract volumes into better shape, organizing the great mass of detailed material so that something publishable could emerge from it.

How plants grow, multiply, and disperse was a source of unending delight for him. "I confess that I love to be convinced of this inextinguishable vitality in Nature," he wrote. "I would rather that my body should be buried in a soil thus wideawake than in a mere inert and dead earth."

A few days later, following an outing to count tree rings, he came

135

down with a severe cold, which rapidly worsened and kept him indoors all winter long. Still, he kept making entries in his journal.

On April 12, 1861, Southern guns bombarded the federal arsenal at Fort Sumter. The Civil War had begun. A week later, forty-five men of Concord, volunteers for Lincoln's Union Army, boarded a train carrying them into the war.

So bad was Thoreau's condition by now that his doctor insisted he must move to a better climate. After considering possible places, he chose Minnesota. It was believed that its dry climate would be beneficial for tuberculosis. (There is no doubt this was his illness.)

So in company with Horace Mann Jr., the young son of the educator, he went by train and steamboat to the West. They were gone

At 4:30 A.M. on April 12, 1861, Confederate batteries opened fire on Fort Sumter, South Carolina, marking the beginning of the American Civil War. At the heart of the war was the conflict over states' rights versus federal authority, with slavery as the keystone issue.

The steamboat Frank Steele, *at right, tied up at the Saint Paul, Minnesota, dock. Thoreau sailed on it some three hundred miles up the Minnesota River with a party of two hundred to visit Indian villages.*

two months, Thoreau all the while making journal entries on what caught his eye—natural history, mostly. Those who met him noted that he spoke with difficulty because of congestion in his chest. In early July, they were back in Concord, Thoreau worse than when he went. As for young Horace Mann, he too would die of tuberculosis, perhaps infected by Thoreau. Consumption, as it was called, was a leading killer in Concord and almost everywhere else.

Late in August, visiting Daniel Ricketson in New Bedford, Massachusetts, Thoreau had his picture taken by the photographer E. S. Dunshee. When it is compared with the daguerreotype (early form of photography) of him made five years earlier in Worcester by Benjamin Maxham, it's shockingly clear how much his illness had aged him. Nevertheless, Thoreau kept working on his natural history projects.

Two images of Thoreau, the Maxham photograph (left) *from 1856, and the Dunshee photograph* (right) *from1861, clearly show the man's deteriorating health. Taken only five years after the Maxham photo, the forty-four-year-old Thoreau in the Dunshee photo looks like an elderly man.*

Fearing what they'd find, Blake and Theophilus Brown came over from Worcester to see how he was doing. They observed that though his body was failing, his spirits were high.

In February 1862, James T. Fields, now the *Atlantic Monthly* editor as well as Thoreau's book publisher, wrote to ask if Thoreau had any essays the magazine could publish. Thoreau knew his family could use the money. So in February and March, he reworked lectures he had given earlier. He sent Fields four pieces: "Autumnal Tints," "Life Without Principle," "Walking," and "Wild Apples."

Fields took them and decided also to buy up the unsold copies of *A Week on the Concord and Merrimack Rivers*. His firm would republish it together with a new edition of *Walden*.

Thoreau knew he was dying. He had not been able to deal with his brother John's death, but now, knowing how near the end was, he accepted his own. He felt that the autumn leaves teach people how to die. The mass deaths of the Civil War, raging on remote battlefields, made one's own death seem incidental.

In his last days, Thoreau's bed was brought down from his attic room and placed in the parlor. Unable to write, he dictated to Sophia. She could hardly hear him for his voice had thinned to a whisper. Friends dropped by. Sam Staples said he had never seen a man "dying with so much pleasure and peace." Someone mentioned Ellen Sewall's name, and Thoreau told Sophia he had always loved her. When his Aunt Louisa asked if he had made his peace with God, he replied, "I did not know we had ever quarreled, Aunt."

Thoreau's grave (left) *is located on Authors' Ridge at the Sleepy Hollow Cemetery in Concord, Massachusetts. His grave and nearby Walden Pond are regularly visited by people inspired by his writings.*

Early in the morning of May 6, as Sophia was helping with the proofreading of *A Week*, Thoreau, listening with pleasure to the final passage of "Friday," where the brothers are nearing home, murmured, "Now comes good sailing." And then, thinking of the book on Maine, he whispered his last words that could be understood—"moose" and "Indian."

He died that morning at nine o'clock. He had lived forty-four years, nine months, and twenty-four days.

A funeral service was held in the First Parish Church, with Emerson reading his eulogy. Concord schools were dismissed so the schoolchildren could follow the funeral procession to Thoreau's grave in the New Burying Ground. Years later, his body was moved to Sleepy Hollow Cemetery.

These are Emerson's last words on his friend Thoreau: "The country knows not yet, or in the least part, how great a son it has lost. . . . Wherever there is knowledge, wherever there is virtue, wherever there is beauty, he will find a home."

Chronology of
Henry David Thoreau

1812	John Thoreau marries Cynthia Dunbar at Concord, Massachusetts.
1812	Helen Thoreau, sister, born at Concord.
1815	John Thoreau Jr., brother, born at Concord.
1817	Henry David Thoreau born July 12 at Concord.
1818	Family moves to Chelmsford, Massachusetts.
1819	Sophia Thoreau, sister, born at Chelmsford.
1821	Family moves to Boston.
1823	Family moves back to Concord. Henry enters school.
1824	Father begins making pencils.
1828	Henry enters Concord Academy.
1833	Henry enters Harvard College.
1834	Ralph Waldo Emerson moves to Concord.
1835	On leave from Harvard, Thoreau teaches school at Canton, Massachusetts.
1836	Goes to New York with father, peddling pencils.
1837	Graduates from Harvard. Begins journal. Teaches briefly in Concord public school.

1838   Makes first trip to Maine. Opens private school in home. Moves school to Concord Academy; brother John becomes preceptor. Delivers his first lecture at Concord Lyceum.

1839   Takes excursion on Concord and Merrimack rivers with brother John. Ellen Sewall visits Concord.

1840   Publishes first essay, "Aulus Persius Flaccus," and first poem, "Sympathy," in the *Dial*. Continues contributing to it until final volume in 1844.

Writes "The Service." Ellen Sewall rejects marriage proposals of both brothers.

1841   Lives at Emerson house for two years. With brother John, takes affirmative in debate at Concord Lyceum on "Is It Ever Proper to Offer Forcible Resistance?"

1842   Brother John dies January 11. Hawthorne moves to Concord.

1843   From now on, Thoreau lectures almost annually at Concord Lyceum. Helps Emerson edit the *Dial*. Begins to contribute to other magazines. Tutors William Emerson's children on Staten Island.

1844   Accidentally sets fire to Concord woods in April. Builds Texas Street house with his father.

1845   Begins building Walden cabin in March. Moves in on July 4. Publishes piece on Wendell Phillips in the *Liberator*.

1846   In July is arrested and put in jail overnight for non-payment of taxes.

Makes trip to Maine woods.

1847   Leaves Walden Pond in September to spend year in Emerson's house while latter lectures in England. Does first professional surveying. Begins collecting natural history specimens for Louis Agassiz at Harvard.

1848   Lectures on January 26 before Concord Lyceum on "The Rights and Duties of the Individual in Relation to Government" (later "Civil Disobedience").

Lectures for first time outside Concord, at Salem, on November 22.

"Ktaadn and the Maine Woods" appears in *Union* magazine. Returns from Emerson's house to live in family's house.

1849   Sister Helen dies June 14. Publishes *A Week on the Concord and Merrimack Rivers*. Meets H. G. O. Blake. "Resistance to Civil Government" (later "Civil Disobedience") appears in *Aesthetic Papers*. In October makes first trip to Cape Cod with Ellery Channing. Lectures in Salem, Massachusetts; Portland, Maine; Worcester, Massachusetts.

1850   Moves to Yellow House at 255 Main Street, where he lives until death.

In June makes second trip to Cape Cod. Hawthorne's *The Scarlet Letter* published.

In September spends week in Canada with Ellery Channing. Lectures at Danvers, Worcester, and Newburyport, Massachusetts. Fugitive Slave Law adopted as part of Compromise of 1850.

1851   Lectures at Clinton, Medford, and Worcester, Massachusetts. Helps fugitive slave escape to Canada.

Melville's *Moby Dick* published.

1852   Lectures at Lincoln, Plymouth, and Boston, Massachusetts.

1853   Makes second trip to Maine woods. Publishes "A Yankee in Canada" in *Putnam's Monthly Magazine*. Family pencil business supplanted by preparation of powdered graphite for electrotyping.

1854   Makes speech, "Slavery in Massachusetts," at July 4 abolitionist meeting in Framingham, Massachusetts. Publishes *Walden* in August. Meets Daniel Ricketson at New Bedford, Massachusetts; Lectures in Plymouth, Massachusetts; Philadelphia, Pennsylvania; Providence, Rhode Island; New Bedford; and Nantucket, Massachusetts.

1855   Visits Cape Cod.

        Publishes part of *Cape Cod* in *Putnam's Monthly Magazine*. Lectures in Worcester, Massachusetts.

        Whitman's *Leaves of Grass* published.

1856   Makes botanical trip to Brattleboro, Vermont. Does surveying and lecturing at Eagleswood and Perth Amboy, New Jersey. Meets Walt Whitman in Brooklyn.

        Lectures in Philadelphia and Amherst, New Hampshire.

1857   Meets abolitionist John Brown in Concord. Walks the length of Cape Cod.

        With Edward Hoar makes last trip to Maine woods. Lectures in Fitchburg and Worcester, Massachusetts.

1858   Publishes "Chesuncook" in *Atlantic Monthly*. Visits the White Mountains and Mount Monadnock. Lectures in Lynn, Massachusetts.

1859	Father dies February 3. After John Brown's capture at Harpers Ferry, delivers "A Plea for Captain John Brown" at Concord, Boston, and Worcester, and, when Brown is executed, delivers "After the Death of John Brown" on December 2 in Concord.
1860	Camps out on Mount Monadnock with Ellery Channing. "A Plea for Captain John Brown" appears in *Echoes of Harpers Ferry*; "The Last Days of John Brown" in the *Liberator*. Lectures on "The Succession of Forest Trees" at the Middlesex Cattle Show. Lectures also in Lowell, Massachusetts and Waterbury, Vermont. Catches cold that brings on his final illness. Lincoln elected president.
1861	American Civil War begins. Makes trip to Minnesota with Horace Mann Jr., May 11 to July 10. Revises many of his manuscripts.
1862	Dies on May 6, at 9:00 A.M., aged forty-four years, nine months, twenty-four days. Buried in New Burying Ground. Years later, his body was moved to Sleepy Hollow Cemetery.
1863	*Excursions* published.
1864	*The Maine Woods* published.
1865	*Cape Cod* published.
1866	*A Yankee in Canada* published.
1906	Journals published in fourteen-volume edition: *The Journals of Henry David Thoreau*.
1993	*Faith in a Seed* published.
2000	*Wild Fruits* published.

Source Notes

Readers should note that many passages from Thoreau's writings referred to are found in Meltzer and Harding, *A Thoreau Profile*. That book attempts a portrait of Thoreau drawn largely in his own words.

14 Milton Meltzer and Walter Harding, *A Thoreau Profile* (New York: The Thoreau Society, 1998), 9.

15 Walter Harding, *The Days of Henry Thoreau: A Biography* (New York: Knopf, 1965), 27.

17 Harding, 31.

20 Robert D. Richardson, *Henry Thoreau: A Life of the Mind* (Berkeley: University of California Press, 1986), 32.

21–23 Meltzer and Harding, 27.

25 Harding, 50.

25 Ibid., 51.

31–32 Harding, 62.

33 Richardson, 72.

34 Harding, 64.

36 Meltzer and Harding, 68.

36 Ibid., 69.

36–37 Ibid., 70.

37 The Thoreau Society, "Great Things Can come from a Journal . . . ," *The Thoreau Reader*, n.d., http://thoreau.eserver.org/journal/html (October 17, 2006).

37–38 Meltzer and Harding, 68.

38 Ibid.

38 Ibid.

38–39 Ibid., 73.

39 Ibid., 75.

43 Harding, 85.

43 Stephen Fink, *Prophet in the Marketplace* (Princeton, NJ: Princeton University Press, 1992), 35.

43 Edward Waldo Emerson, *Henry Thoreau As Remembered by a Young Friend* (Boston: Houghton Mifflin, 1917), 128.

44 Richardson, 389.

44 Ibid.

47 Emerson, 56.

52 Harding, 138.

52 Fink, 56.

54 Harding, 76.

55 Ibid., 79.

56 Ibid., 149.

57 Meltzer and Harding, 82.

59 Ibid., 86.

59–60 Ibid., 87.

62 Todd R. Felton, "An Early Naturalist Burns Down a Concord Forest," *ConcordMA.com*, n.d., http://www.concordma.com/magazine/autumn06/transcendentalists.html (October 20, 2006).

63 Harding, 173.

64 Ibid., 175.

73 Harding,191.

73 Ibid., 186.

74 Ibid., 196.

75 Richardson, 171.

76 Meltzer and Harding, 158.

78 Milton Meltzer, *Bound for the Rio Grande: The Mexican Struggle 1845–1850* (New York: Knopf, 1974), 114.

78 Ibid., 336.

78 Meltzer and Harding, 162.

80 Meltzer, 116.

84–85 Meltzer and Harding, 165–167.

86 Meltzer and Harding, 172.

88 Ibid., 135.

88 Ibid., 126.

89 Fink, 200.

89 Ibid., 269.

89–90 Richardson,188.

90–91 Fink, 194.

92–93 Meltzer and Harding, 157.

94 Harding, 228.

95 Ibid., 239.

96 Richardson, 187.

97 Fink, 245.

97 Ibid.

98 Meltzer and Harding, 180.

100 Fink, 254.

102 Richardson, 201.

102 Meltzer and Harding, 289.

106 Harding, 407.

108 Henry David Thoreau, *Walking*. (Kila, MT: Kessinger Publishing, 2004), part II.

110 Meltzer and Harding, 196.

111–112 Ibid., 199–200.

112–113 Ibid., 200.

144 Ibid., 201.

115 Peter J. Bellis, *Writing Revolution: Aesthetics and Politics in Hawthorne, Whitman, and Thoreau* (Athens: University of Georgia Press, 2003), 146.

116 Ibid., 147.

116 Ibid., 148.

116 Ibid.

118–119 Meltzer and Harding, 250–251.

119 Whitman, Walt. *Leaves of Grass*. (Philadelphia: David McKay, 1900), 100.

120 Michael Sperber, *Henry David Thoreau: Cycles and Psyche* (Higganum, CT: Higganum Hill Books, 2004), 83.

120 Richardson, 332.

120 Bradford Torrey and Frances Allen, eds., *Reading The Journal of Henry David Thoreau*, vol. 6, (New York: Dover, 1962), 773.

121 Meltzer and Harding, 234.

122 Harding, 334.

123 Thoreau Institute at Walden Woods, *"Contemporary Notices and Reviews of* Walden; or, Life in the Woods," n.d., http://www .walden.org/Institute/thoreau/ writings/walden/Reviews/ Oneida%20Circular%201%20 August%201854. htm, (September 4, 2006).

123 Thoreau Institute at Walden Woods, *"Contemporary Notices and Reviews of* Walden; or, Life in the Woods," n.d., http://www .walden.org/Institute/thoreau/ writings/walden/Reviews/ Daily%20Evening%20 Traveller%209%20August% 201854.htm, (September 4, 2006).

123 Thoreau Institute at Walden Woods, *"Contemporary Notices and Reviews of* Walden; or, Life in the Woods," n.d., http://www.walden .org/Institute/thoreau/ writings/walden/Reviews/ Boston%20Daily%20Bee% 209%20August%201854.htm, (September 4, 2006).

124 Langston Hughes and Milton Meltzer, *A Pictorial History of African Americans* (New York: Crown, 1995), 46.

126 Meltzer and Harding, 246.

126–127 Ibid., 255.

128 Harding, 413.

130–131 Herbert Aptheker, *John Brown: American Martyr* (New York: New Century, 1960), 9.

130–131 Herbert

131 Hughes and Meltzer, 150.

132 Hughes and Meltzer, 153.

132 Ibid

132 Ibid

132 Ibid

132 Ibid

132 Ibid

133 Richardson, 372.

133–134 Ibid.

135 Richardson, 385.

139 Meltzer and Harding, 288.

140 Harding, 466.

140 Ibid., 467.

Bibliography

Bellis, Peter J. *Writing Revolution: Aesthetics and Politics in Hawthorne, Whitman, and Thoreau*. Athens: University of Georgia Press, 2003.

Bennett, Jane. *Thoreau's Nature: Ethics, Politics, and the Wild*. Lanham, MD: Rowman & Littlefield, 2000.

Cain, William E. *A Historical Guide to Henry David Thoreau*. New York: Oxford University Press, 2000.

Dean, Bradley D. *Henry David Thoreau: Letters to a Spiritual Seeker*. New York: Norton, 2004.

Emerson, Edward Waldo. *Henry Thoreau As Remembered by a Young Friend*. Boston: Houghton Mifflin, 1917.

Fink, Stephen. *Prophet in the Marketplace*. Princeton, NJ: Princeton University Press, 1992.

Harding, Walter. *The Days of Henry Thoreau: A Biography*. New York: Knopf, 1965; Dover, 1982.

Harding, Walter, ed. *Thoreau As Seen by His Contemporaries*. New York: Dover, 1989.

Howarth, William L. *The Book of Concord: Thoreau's Life as a Writer*. New York: Viking, 1982.

Photo Acknowledgments

The images in this book are used with the permission of: Library of Congress, pp. 2 (LC-USZ61-361), 33 (LC-USZ62-39828), 54 (LC-DIG-ppmsca-08322), 65 (LC-DIG-cwpbh-03684), 121 (LC-USZ62-90560), 138 right (LC-USZ61-361); Courtesy Concord Free Public Library, pp. 11, 12 (both), 13, 29 (top), 32, 41, 46, 49, 55, 62, 63, 66, 76, 77, 79, 87 (top), 88, 90, 91, 94, 96, 97, 101, 108, 111, 115, 133, 139; © Getty Images, pp. 18, 22, 23, 30, 47, 56, 82, 105, 130, 131, 132, 136, 138 (left); © Brown Brothers, p. 20; Emerson Society Quarterly, p. 24; © Roger Viollet Collection/Getty Images, p. 27; Abernethy Collection, Special Collections, Middlebury College, Middlebury, Vermont, p. 29 (bottom); The Pierpont Morgan Library, New York. MA 1303, p. 37; Courtesy of the Thoreau Society Collections, p. 42; National Park Service, Longfellow National Historic Site, p. 53; Cornell University Library, Making of America Digital Collection, p. 58; Massachusetts Historical Society, p. 69; © David Muench/CORBIS, p. 70; © Prisma/Superstock, p. 71; Photo by David Bohl, Concord Museum, Concord, MA, p. 85; Henry W. and Albert A. Berg Collection of English and American Literature, The New York Public Library, Astor, Lenox and Tilden Foundations, p. 87 (bottom); General Research Division, The New York Public Library, Astor Lenox and Tilden Foundations, p. 98; Henry David Thoreau Herbarium, Botany Libraries, Harvard University, Cambridge, MA, p. 103; Todd-Bingham Picture Collection. Manuscripts and Archives, Yale University Library, p. 114; Courtesy of the Bahley-Whitman Collection of Ohio Wesleyan University, p. 118; © North Wind Picture Archive, p. 125; William Henry Illingworth, Minnesota Historical Society, p. 137.

Cover image © Getty Images